J. N. Fradenburgh

Beauty crowned

The story of Esther, The Jewish Maiden

J. N. Fradenburgh

Beauty crowned

The story of Esther, The Jewish Maiden

ISBN/EAN: 9783337101428

Printed in Europe, USA, Canada, Australia, Japan

Cover: Foto ©Lupo / pixelio.de

More available books at **www.hansebooks.com**

OR,

THE STORY OF ESTHER,

THE JEWISH MAIDEN.

BY

REV. J. N. FRADENBURGH, Ph.D., D.D.,

Member of the American Oriental Society, the Society of Biblical Archæology of London, etc.

Author of "Witnesses from the Dust," etc.

———

NEW YORK:
PHILLIPS & HUNT.
CINCINNATI:
CRANSTON & STOWE.
1887.

TO

THE QUEENLY WOMEN OF AMERICA,

THE LIGHT OF HOME,

THE INSPIRATION OF PATRIOTISM,

THE HEART OF RELIGION, THE LIFE OF REFORM,

THIS VOLUME IS

Worshipfully Inscribed.

PREFACE.

THE story of Esther possesses a charm peculiarly its own. The style is perfect and the Hebrew pure. There are only enough Persian words to give it an Oriental flavor, and only enough later Hebrew to suit the date of its composition. There is no affectation, and the only art is the unconscious "art of artlessness." There is no attempt at the sublime, yet the book is not lacking in sublimity. The characters stand out in clear light and speak for themselves. There is no waste of words, yet the whole story is told. Each part fills its own proper place, and the skillfully-planned denouement is most dramatic. It is altogether a magnificent piece of writing which never fails to fascinate the reader.

The Book of Esther is an important chapter in the history of the world, and its story moves in the midst of stirring events. The impartial student cannot well afford to neglect this priceless contribution. The deliverance of the people of God from the fury of Haman the Agagite should be mentioned with the earlier deliverance from Egyptian bondage.

This story furnishes glimpses of the court of a Persian king, his harem, and his palace; it refers to many customs connected with social and domestic life; it portrays the character of an Oriental despot and outlines the organization of his government; and it proclaims the queenliness of a beautiful woman when possessed of corresponding graces of mind and heart. The story touches history at so many points, and the references to laws and customs—many of them undesigned—are so numerous, that it were easy to detect a mistake, if the writer were not true to facts.

In the present work the author has so woven classical and Oriental illustrations into the story that the minute truthfulness of the account may be considered demonstrated beyond successful controversy. The reader will feel confident that it is not mere romance but veritable history, while the charm of the story is greatly heightened by this consideration.

The questions of temperance and home, brought prominently forward, have received a fair share of consideration, while other lesser but important subjects have not been forgotten.

It is believed that this new dress in which the story of Esther appears will insure new interest in its study.

July, 1887.

CONTENTS.

CHAPTER	PAGE
I. The Vast Kingdom and the Mighty King	9
II. The Magnificent Palace	24
III. The Banquet of Wine	46
IV. Folly, Anger, Divorce	80
V. Love and Home	96
VI. The Queenliness of Beauty	107
VII. Enthroned and Crowned	129
VIII. The Conspiracy Discovered	141
IX. Pride Before a Fall	147
X. Superstition and Cruelty, Hand in Hand	157
XI. Suspense, Agony, Resolution	176
XII. Magnificent Heroism, Masterly Delay, Wakeful Providence	192
XIII. Wheels Within Wheels	205
XIV. Poetic Justice	216
XV. The Beginning of the End	224
XVI. Victory, Peace, Gladness	235
XVII. Prosperity, Happiness	247
Index	257

Illustrations.

	PAGE
TESSELATED PAVEMENTS	38
PERSIAN KING	49
ROYAL PARASOL	56
KING WITH ATTENDANTS	57
FAN, OR FLY-CHASER	57
SCENT-BOTTLE	58
JEWISH CAPTIVES	108
JUDEA CAPTA	112
ARTICLES FOR THE TOILET	130
EAR-DROPS	132
NECK COLLARS	132
BRACELETS	135
ARMLETS	136
ORIENTAL PROSTRATION	154
SEAL-RINGS	169
KING ON HIS THRONE	193
IMPALEMENT	223
ORDINARY PERSIAN COSTUME	230
SUBJECTS BRING TRIBUTE TO THE KING	249
THE TOMB OF MORDECAI AND ESTHER	254

BEAUTY CROWNED.

I.

THE VAST KINGDOM AND THE MIGHTY KING.

"Ahasuerus which reigned from India even unto Ethiopia, over an hundred and seven and twenty provinces."—ESTHER i, 1.

SENNACHERIB is the most colossal figure in all Assyrian history, in whom more than in any other monarch were impersonated Oriental pride, violence, and power. He defeated a host of Ethiopians and Egyptians at Ekron, and, in order to restore the Ekronite king, who had been deposed and sent to Hezekiah, invaded Judea and took forty-six fenced cities, and of smaller cities and towns "a countless number." Hezekiah sued for peace, and despoiled the temple to pay the heavy tribute imposed by the conqueror. Expecting help from Egypt, he again revolted, and Sennacherib sent him a stern letter demanding unconditional and immediate surrender.

The letter was spread before Him who was enthroned above the cherubim, and he answered Sennacherib: "I will put my hook in thy nose, and my bridle in thy lips, and I will turn thee back by the way by which thou camest." 2 Kings xix, 28. The morning brought these tidings to Jerusalem: "The angel of the Lord went out, and smote in the camp of the Assyrians an hundred fourscore and five thousand." 2 Kings xix, 35.

In the reign of Assurbanipal, grandson of Sennacherib, Assyria reached her highest glory. "Behold, the Assyrian was a cedar in Lebanon with fair branches, and with a shadowing shroud, and of an high stature; and his top was among the thick boughs. The waters made him great, the deep set him up on high with her rivers running round about his plants, and sent out her little rivers unto all the trees of the field. Therefore his height was exalted above all the trees of the field, and his boughs were multiplied, and his branches became long because of the multitude of waters, when he shot forth. All the fowls of heaven made their nests in his boughs, and under his branches did all the beasts of the field bring forth their young, and under his shadow dwelt all great nations. Thus was he fair in his greatness, in the length of his branches: for his root was by great waters. The cedars of the garden of God could not hide him: the fir-trees were not like his boughs, and the chestnut-trees were not like his branches; not any tree in the garden of God was like unto him in his beauty. I have made him fair by the multitude of his branches; so that all the trees of Eden, that were in the garden of God, envied him." Ezek. xxxi, 3–9.

The Medes and Babylonians invaded the kingdom, and the cedar fell in B.C. 625.

Nebuchadnezzar was the grandest figure in Babylonian history. His siege of Tyre, which lasted thirteen years, was most memorable. He laid siege to Jerusalem, which endured untold horrors and resisted with the energy of despair, but after eighteen months yielded to the resistless fury of the proud conqueror.

By the naked physical strength of his captives he was enabled to construct those gigantic works—the great wall of Babylon, the "hanging gardens," magnificent palaces, canals, a vast reservoir, quays and breakwaters, temples and embankments—which have done far more to render his name illustrious than all his military exploits. Near the close of his reign he was attacked by a strange malady known to the physicians as lycanthropy. He believed himself a beast; fled the society of men, discarded clothing, fed on herbs, and became covered with a shaggy coat of hair. After "seven times" he was restored, and praised the God of heaven. He died B.C. 561.

Cyaxares founded the Median kingdom, and shared with Nabopolassar of Babylon the territory of the conquered Assyrians. He sought occasion to make war against most ancient, proud, and unconquered Lydia, a kingdom whose river Pactolus ran with gold, whose people invented coined money, and whose king Gyges was celebrated for his wars, his wealth, and the romance of his history. The war was waged with great fury and varying success. At length, while the two armies were engaged in deadly conflict, darkness fell upon both—it was an eclipse of the sun—and struck all with awe and terror.

They cease to fight and contemplate the portent. They agree upon an armistice and arrange terms of peace. The two monarchs meet, repeat the terms of the treaty, pierce their arms, and seal the contract by sucking each the other's blood.

Media was conquered by Cyrus B.C. 558. "The mighty one of the heathen" and the "terrible of the nations,". after an existence of sixty-seven years, passed away.

Xerxes inherited the broadest empire of kingdoms the world had ever seen—"from India even unto Ethiopia." He was assassinated in his sleeping apartment B.C. 465. At the battle of Arbela, B.C. 330, "the crown of Cyrus passed to the Macedonian."

The Persians were "quick and lively, keen-witted, capable of repartee, ingenious, and, for Orientals, far-sighted." They had fancy and imagination, but with the exuberance of the imaginative faculty there were childishness, extravagance, and grotesqueness. They had a relish for poetry, and the writings of their bards, with much that is pretty, sparkling, and quaint, are full of Oriental marvels. They were bold and warlike, and in courage stood at the head of the nations of their time. The Greeks defeated them not because of superior bravery in battle, but because of better arms, better equipment, more perfect organization, and severer discipline. The Persians certainly possessed more stubbornness in conflict and more endurance than any neighboring nation. They were endowed with great energy, and waged war after war and conducted expedition after expedition with little rest, enjoying a career of conquest which has few parallels in history. Falsehood was considered the basest of sins, and self-indulgence and luxury were unknown. Persians were immoderate in the manifestation of joy or sorrow, and "laughed and wept, shouted and shrieked, with the unrestraint of children who are not ashamed to lay bare their inmost feelings to the eyes of those about them. Lively and excitable, they loved to give vent to every passion that stirred their hearts, and cared not how many witnessed their lamentations or their rejoicings."

The king had absolute control over the property, liberty, and lives of his subjects, and none dared dispute his will. His empire was eight times as large as the Babylonian and four times as large as the Assyrian at their widest sway.

There was nothing in Persia proper to prophesy so magnificent a growth and so glorious a history. It was but one twentieth of the size of the empire in its glory. The warm district of Fars, about one eighth of the whole in area, extends between the mountains and the sea the whole length of the province; a narrow strip of land, of poor, sandy, and clayey soil, poorly watered, of torrid heat, unpropitious and unproductive. The remainder of the province, though generally sterile and barren, contains not a few richly fertile sections, "picturesque and romantic almost beyond imagination, with lovely wooded dells, green mountain sides, and broad plains suited for the production of almost any crop." It is poorly watered, the few rivers being generally lost in the sands or salt lakes. The mountain gorges afford the most remarkable feature of the country. Scarped rocks rise sheer on either side of mountain streams sometimes to a height of two thousand feet. Roads are cut on the sides of the precipices, and pass by bridges from side to side over profound chasms, through which angry streams dash and roar and chafe and foam, leaping many a cascade, and fall, restless and furious, rushing to the sea. The country is strongly defended on the north and east by deserts, and on the south by a strong mountain wall.

The provinces of the Persian monarchy are those which have made the history of the Oriental world.

There is Babylonia, with its great cities, its most ancient literature, its idolatrous worship, its magicians and astrologers, its magnificence and wealth, the home of Abraham and the land of the Jewish captivity. There is Assyria, with its bloody Nineveh, its temples, its fertility, its conquests, its pride, its unspeakable cruelties, its kings, and its mighty hunters—the land of the captivity of the ten tribes of Israel. There is Susiana, with its ancient Accadian race and religion, and its magnificent court in "Shushan the palace." There is Asia Minor, with its classic streams, its great nations, its Ionic cities, and its Homeric sites. There are Cyprus, whose rich mines gave the name of copper, *cyprium*, to the civilized world, and Armenia, the traditional land of the Noachian Ararat. There is Phenicia, one of the pioneer nations in letters and commerce, with its Tyre and Sidon, and its many distant colonies. There is Palestine, the Land of Promise, flowing with milk and honey—the land of the chosen people of God—with its sacred cities, holy shrines, and wonderful history. There is Egypt, the land of the pyramid and the tomb, the obelisk and the sphinx, the idol and the temple, the land of the most ancient hieroglyphic literature, the land of the proud Pharaohs, and of Joseph and Moses, of the famine, the plague, and the pestilence. There are Aria, the primitive home of the Aryan race, and Bactria, the home of Zoroaster. And there is India, of inexhaustible resources, of prodigious literature, and of a religion having the most cumbrous ritual of any religion in the world—India promising a most glorious future.

The account given of the character of Ahasuerus is a life-like picture of a Persian king, and especially of Xerxes as presented by our best authorities. There is abundant proof of this statement.

The story of Cambyses is characteristic. His cupbearer was the son of Prexaspes, and Prexaspes had offended the king by telling him that the Persians thought him too much given to wine. Cambyses replied: "'Judge now thyself, Prexaspes, whether the Persians tell the truth, or whether it is not they who are mad for speaking as they do. Look there, now, at thy son standing in the vestibule; if I shoot and hit him right in the middle of the heart, it will be plain the Persians have no grounds for what they say; if I miss him, then I allow that the Persians are right, and that I am out of my mind.' So speaking, he drew the bow to the full and struck the boy, who straightway fell down dead. Then Cambyses ordered the body to be opened, and the wound examined; and, when the arrow was found to have entered the heart, the king was quite overjoyed, and said to the father, with a laugh, 'Now thou seest plainly, Prexaspes, that it is not I who am mad, but the Persians who have lost their senses. I pray thee, tell me, sawest thou ever mortal man send an arrow with a better aim?' Prexaspes, seeing that the king was not in his right mind, and fearing for himself, replied, 'O my lord! I do not think that God himself could shoot so dexterously.' Such was the outrage which Cambyses committed at this time; at another, he took twelve of the noblest Persians, and, without bringing any charge worthy of death against them, buried them all up to the neck." *

Herodotus relates that Cambyses entered the royal palace at Saïs, and caused the body of King Amasis to be brought from the sepulcher, scourged, pricked with goads, and subjected to all manner of insult. Having in this inhuman manner satisfied his rage, he ordered its burial.

Crœsus, the Lydian, gave Cambyses valuable advice, but was repaid with the sentence to death. The servants charged with his execution concealed the conquered king, believing that Cambyses would soon repent of his impulsive wickedness. It turned out as they anticipated, but when Cambyses was informed that Crœsus was alive, he replied, "I am glad that Crœsus lives, but as for you who saved him, ye shall not escape my vengeance, but shall all of you be put to death." So saying, he caused them all to be slain.†

Astyages had a dream which prophesied ruin to

* Herodotus, iii, 35.   † *Ibid*, iii, 36.

himself, but honor to Cyrus, the infant son of his daughter Mandané. Moved by terror, he gave Cyrus to Harpagus to be slain. Some time after this, he learned that Cyrus had been spared, and rejoiced, but "took the son of Harpagus, and slew him, after which he cut him in pieces, and roasted some pieces before the fire, and boiled others," and served up to Harpagus the cannibal food at a banquet. Then, asking his guest how he enjoyed the repast, he showed him the head, hands, and feet of his son.

When Cyrus reached the Gyndes with his army, one of his sacred white horses—the story may be a fable—was swept away by the swift current and drowned. "Cyrus, enraged at the insolence of the river, threatened so to break its strength that in future even women should cross it easily without wetting their knees." Thereupon he dispersed the stream through three hundred and sixty channels.*

This inconsistent, despotic, and savage trait of character was prominent in Xerxes. When a great storm broke the first bridge which he threw across the Hellespont, he "straightway gave orders that the Hellespont should receive three hundred lashes, and that a pair of fetters should be cast into it. Nay, I have even heard it said that he bade the branders take their irons, and therewith brand the Hellespont." Those who scourged the waters uttered at his com-

* Herodotus, i, 119, 189, 190.

mand these words: "Thou bitter water, thy lord lays on thee this punishment because thou hast wronged him without a cause, having suffered no evil at his hands. Verily, King Xerxes will cross thee, whether thou wilt or no. Well dost thou deserve that no man should honor thee with sacrifice; for thou art of a truth a treacherous and unsavory river." He also ordered them who had constructed the bridge to be put to death.*

Before the battle of Salamis, which decided the fate of Greece, Artemisia advised him not to risk an engagement at sea, and so well was the character of Xerxes known that the friends of the noble and warlike queen feared for her life. During the progress of the battle certain Phenicians whose ships had been sunk accused the Ionians of being traitors. Just then the gallant conduct of a Samothracian vessel contradicted their words. "Xerxes, when he saw the exploit, turned fiercely on the Phenicians (he was ready, in his extreme vexation, to find fault with any one), and ordered their heads to be cut off, to prevent them, he said, from casting the blame of their own misconduct upon braver men." After the battle, Mardonius feared the king's vengeance for having advised the ill-fated expedition.†

In his retreat from Europe Xerxes embarked in a Phenician vessel. A storm arose, the ship labored

* Herodotus, vii, 35. † *Ibid.*, viii, 69, 90, 100.

heavily, and the helmsman despaired of saving the king, unless he could get "quit of these too numerous passengers." Whereupon the king, addressing the Persians, said, "Men of Persia, now is the time for you to show what love you bear your king. My safety, as it seems, depends wholly upon you." The Persians of his train "instantly made obeisance, and then leaped over into the sea." The ship was lightened, and the king saved. When Xerxes reached the shore he gave the helmsman a golden crown because he had saved his life, "but, because he had caused the death of a number of Persians, he ordered his head to be struck from his shoulders." This account, however, is not credited by Herodotus, and yet, as Rawlinson says, it is "a striking embodiment of the real Oriental feeling with regard to the person of the monarch." *

At another time we see him in a different mood. When he looked out upon the Hellespont, covered with his immense fleet ready to proceed upon its career of expected conquest, he wept at the sight. When asked the cause of his weeping, he replied: "There came upon me a sudden pity when I thought of the shortness of man's life, and considered that of all this host, so numerous as it is, not one will be alive when a hundred years are gone by." †

Like other Persian kings, Xerxes met with many

* Herodotus, viii, 118. † *Ibid.,* vii, 46.

difficulties in his amours which resulted in rage, cruelty, and murder. The story of his love of Artaÿnta, the daughter of Masistes, his brother, will be related in a future chapter.

Rawlinson sums up the character of Xerxes: "The character of Xerxes falls below that of any preceding monarch. Excepting that he was not wholly devoid of a certain magnanimity, which made him listen patiently to those who opposed his views, or gave him unpalatable advice, and which prevented him from exacting vengeance on some occasions, he had scarcely a trait whereon the mind can rest with any satisfaction. Weak and easily led, puerile in his gusts of passion, and his complete abandonment of himself to them—selfish, fickle, boastful, cruel, superstitious, licentious—he exhibits to us the Oriental despot in the most contemptible of all his aspects—that wherein the moral and the intellectual qualities are equally in defect, and the career is one unvarying course of vice and folly. From Xerxes we have to date at once the decline of the empire in respect of territorial greatness and military strength, and likewise its deterioration in regard to administrative vigor and national spirit. With him commenced the corruption of the court—the fatal evil which almost universally weakens and destroys Oriental dynasties. His expedition against Greece exhausted and depopulated the empire; and though, by abstaining from further military enterprises, he did what lay in his power to recruit its strength, still the losses which his expedition caused were certainly not repaired in his life-time." He may, however, be placed "in the foremost rank of Oriental builders." *

The character of Ahasuerus fits no Persian monarch so well as Xerxes, and it fits him exactly. The name is the same. The transliteration of Ahasuerus, Achashverosh of the Hebrew, Khshayarsha of the cuneiform inscriptions, and Xerxes is very close, and no other transliteration is possible. The extent of the empire suits the reign of this monarch. He reigned "from India even unto Ethiopia, *over* an hundred and seven and twenty provinces." According to Daniel, Darius the Mede set over his kingdom a hundred and twenty satraps. Dan. vi, 2. Herodotus says that Darius divided the kingdom into twenty satrapies, but each of these embraced several geographical regions or "provinces." Mardonius names Indians and Ethiopians as subjects of Xerxes. They paid tribute to Persia, and served in the mighty army.†

In an inscription of Xerxes, at Persepolis, he calls himself "sole king of many kings, sole emperor of many emperors." He says: "I am Xerxes, the great king, the king of kings, the king of the lands where

---

* Rawlinson, *Ancient Monarchies*, vol. iii, pp. 470, 471.
† Herodotus, iii, 9, 65, 69, 70; vii, 94, 97, 98.

many languages are spoken, the king of this wide earth, afar and near." *

The chronology of events is perfectly harmonious, while the history of no other Persian monarch can be made to harmonize with the Book of Esther.

"In the third year of the reign of Xerxes was held an assembly to arrange the Grecian war; † in the third year of Ahasuerus was held a great feast and assembly in Shushan the palace. Esth. i, 3. In the seventh year of his reign Xerxes returned defeated from Greece, and consoled himself by the pleasures of the harem; ‡ in the seventh year of his reign 'fair young virgins were sought' for Ahasuerus, and he replaced Vashti by marrying Esther. The tribute he 'laid upon the land, and upon the isles of the sea' (Esth. x, 1) may well have been the result of the expenditure and ruin of the Grecian expedition." §

We may consider the identification of Ahasuerus with Xerxes as settled beyond all dispute. His name, his character, his place in history, and the events themselves are fully satisfied by this identification.

---

* Oppert, *Records of the Past*, vol. ix, p. 81.
† Herodotus, vii, 7, *sq.* ‡ *Ibid.*, ix, 108.
§ McClintock and Strong's Cyclopedia, Ahasuerus.

II.

THE MAGNIFICENT PALACE.

"Shushan the palace."—ESTHER i, 2.

SUSA, "the city of lilies," "ornate with the gold of Cissia," was the capital of the biblical Elam, the Elymais of the geographers, the Cissia of the Greeks, the Susis or Susiana of the later Greeks. "This territory comprised a portion of the mountain country which separates Mesopotamia from Persia; but is chiefly composed of the broad and rich flats intervening between the mountains and the Tigris, along the courses of the Kerkhah, Kuran, and Jerahi rivers. It was a rich and fertile tract, resembling Chaldea in its general character," while "the vicinity of the mountains lent it freshness, giving it cooler streams, more frequent rains, and pleasanter breezes." *

The mountains of Luristan furnish prominent features in the appearance of the country. "The great range attains an elevation of eight or ten thousand feet above the sea, and bears in a general direction toward the north-west. Its rocky masses belong entirely to the cetaceous and lower tertiary series, rising in huge, elongated saddles of compact altered

---

* Rawlinson, *Ancient Monarchies*, vol. i, p. 26.

limestone parallel to each other. At intervals, where the elevating force which produced the present configuration of this region has acted with extreme intensity, the continuity of the beds became broken, and masses of rock were left standing isolated, with precipitous escarpments, presenting retreats accessible only to the savage inhabitants. 'Diz' is the name applied to natural fortresses of this kind, which frequently bear on their summits acres of rich grass and springs of delicious water, whither a native chief with his adherents can retire in safety in times of need, and defend their difficult passes with a handful of men against the whole power of the Persian government itself.

"Superimposed on the harder limestone rocks are beds of a softer nature—marls, rivaling the colored sands of our own Isle of Wight in their brilliant and variegated aspect; vast piles of amorphous gypsum dazzling the eye with its excessive whiteness, and successive layers of red sands alternating with gravel. These formations follow the contortions of the harder crystalline limestones, lie at extraordinary angles on the slopes of the saddles, and fill up the hot, feverish valleys between them. Wherever the highlands of Persia are approached from the plains of Mesopotamia, the same formidable barrier of mountains presents itself. To attain the high level of that garden of roses, which the Persian poet loves to descant on, it is necessary to climb the successive ridges by roads scarcely better than goat tracks, which regular gradation of ascents is approximately described by the Greek historians as *klimakes* or 'ladders.' All the great rivers which flow from the east into the Tigris have their sources in these mountains, crossing diagonally through the intricacies of the chain. Instead of flowing in a south-east direction, along the trough which separates two parallel limestone saddles, and by this means working out its channel in the soft rocks of the gypsiferous and marly series, and rounding the extremity of the saddle where it dips under the overlying deposits, each of these rivers takes a direction at right angles to its former course, and passes directly through the limestone range by means of a 'tang,' or gorge, apparently formed for this express purpose. On reaching the next succeeding gypsum trough, it follows its original south-east course for a short distance, and again crosses the next chain in the same manner, until it attains the verdant plains of Assyria, or Susiana. Many of these tangs expose a perpendicular section of one thousand feet and upward, and were formed, not by the scooping process which attends river action, but by natural rents produced by the tension of the crystalline mass at the period of its elevation."[*]

From the mountains of Susiana the Accadians de-

[*] Loftus, *Chaldea and Susiana*, pp. 308, 309.

scended, and settled in the plains of Chaldea. Susa, the capital, was on "an open gravel plain about thirty miles from the mountains." Three hundred and fifty miles north-west of Susa is Nizir, the Chaldean Ararat. "Nowhere have I seen," says Mr. Loftus, "such rich vegetation as that which clothes the verdant plains of Shúsh, interspersed with numerous plants of a sweet-scented and delicate iris." * This flower is one of those called "lily" by the Orientals—it is the *Iris sisyrynchium*, L. The purple is the royal color of Persia, and it has been thought that the abundance of these flowers gave the name of "Shushan" to this locality. The Hebrew *Shōshän*, Arabic *Susan*, means any large bright flower. There are others, however, who suppose that Shushan is a Pehlevi word and means "pleasant," and the neighboring city called Shuster means "more pleasant." This "city of lilies," or "pleasant city," occupied a most beautiful spot. The great mound which marks the site of its citadel rises one hundred and twenty feet above the Shapur. The "tomb of Daniel" is on the west, and the forsaken bed of the Eulæus, the "river Ulaï" of the Bible, on the east.

"It is difficult to conceive a more imposing sight than Susa, as it stood in the days of its Kayanian splendor—its great citadel and columnar edifices raising their stately heads above groves of date,

* Loftus, *Chaldea and Susiana*, p. 346.

konar, and lemon-trees, surrounded by rich pastures and golden seas of corn, and backed by the distant snow-clad mountains. Neither Babylon nor Persepolis could compare with Susa in position—watered by her noble rivers, producing crops without irrigation, clothed with grass in spring, and within a moderate journey of a delightful summer clime. Susa vied with Babylon in the riches which the Euphrates conveyed to her stores, while Persepolis must have been inferior, both in point of commercial position and picturesque appearance." *

The heat of summer is very great at Susa. The Greek geographer relates that "lizards and serpents at midday in the summer, when the sun is at its greatest height, cannot cross the streets of the city quick enough to prevent their being burned to death midway by the heat."† The lizards of the country attract the attention of the traveler. Mr. Loftus says: "Clinging to the rocks, basking in the hot sun, or fleetly pursuing smaller reptiles, were numerous huge lizards (*Psammosaurus scincus*), lashing their long tails and opening their capacious black jaws. . . . They live chiefly on snakes, which they pounce on suddenly, shake as a terrier does a rat, and cranch from tail to head; then they suck the mangled body down their throats, somewhat after the manner of a

---

* Loftus, *Chaldea and Susiana*, p. 347.
† Strabo, vol. iii, p. 134.

Neapolitan swallowing his national macaroni! I once saw a lizard of this species attack, kill, and attempt to swallow a serpent six feet long. After gulping for a length of time to get down the tip end of its victim's tail, which hung out of its mouth, it disgorged its meal, repeated the process of mastication, and ultimately, after some hard gasping, succeeded in overcoming its difficulty."*

Ancient inscriptions are to be found among the ruins of Susa. In Genesis, Elam is the first born of Shem. Twice in the fourteenth chapter we find the title "king of Elam" given to Chedorlaomer. Ezra makes Elamites dependents of the Persian empire. Long afterward they appeared among the company which gathered in the upper room on the day of Pentecost.

Modern research has revealed a great kingdom. In the providence of God this old kingdom has had its resurrection. Elam is thought to be a translation of the old Accadian name of Susiana, and means "highland." The Babylonians, according to traditions from the monuments, were oppressed by the Elamites under Khumbaba, but were delivered by the hero Izdubar, whom the late George Smith identifies with Nimrod. There are other traces of the early power of Elam. When Assurbanipal conquered the country, and took Susa, B. C. 645, he brought

* Loftus, *Chaldea and Susiana*, p. 306.

back an image of the goddess Nana which Kudur Nakkhunti had carried away when he overran Babylonia, B. C. 2280. Again, Kudur-Mabug, king of Elam, carried his conquests as far as Phenicia, and assumed the titles "Lord of Phenicia" and "Lord of Elam." His son Eriaku, *Arioch*, was king of Larsa, *Ellasar*. The land of Shinar, or Sumir of the inscriptions, was under the Septuagint King Amarphal, a name which has been recovered in Amarpal. The Goïm, *Guti* or *Gutium* of the inscriptions, at least a part of them, became the Assyrians of later times. Their king was Tidal, Septuagint Thargal, Accadian *Tur-gal*, or "great chief." Kudur-Mabug is probably Chedorlaomer. He was overlord of the allied kings, mentioned above, when he extended his conquests to Phenicia, and was defeated by Abraham. Thus the names of old potentates rising from the mists of remote antiquity furnish a most powerful confirmation of the Bible records. Elam has demonstrated her right to an historic place among the nations of Oriental antiquity.

Susa was a rival of Nineveh at an early period, and under the Achæmenian dynasty usurped the greatness of both Nineveh and Babylon. Cleomenes, king of Sparta, wished to engage Aristagoras as an ally of the Ionians against Darius. The Spartan king, in a remarkable speech, said: "Susa, where the Persian monarch occasionally resides, and where his treasures are deposited — make yourself master of this city and you may vie in influence with Jupiter himself." Alexander the Great, after the battle of Arbela, made Susa the depository of the wealth which he had gathered from the conquered world. Upon entering Susa, Alexander found in the treasury immense sums of money, fifty thousand talents of silver in ore and ingots and five thousand quintals of Hermione purple. After this the city maintained its importance for more than nine hundred years, when it was finally deserted in favor of other rising cities.

The Kerkhah, or Choaspes, a noble stream near the ancient city, is noted for its pure and sparkling water. It is said that the Persian kings would drink no other, and when on warlike expeditions carried water from this royal stream.* Milton sings of its purity:

> "There Susa by Choaspes' amber stream,
> The drink of none but kings."

The rivers, Kerkhah on the west, and the Dizfúl on the east—the Choaspes and the Coprates of the ancients—approach within two and a quarter miles of a junction. At the point of their nearest approximation stand the mounds of Shúsh, three and a half miles in circumference, or, if various smaller mounds are included, covering the whole visible plain of Sháour. A branch of the Dizfúl is the Shapur, or

* Herodotus, i, 188.

Eulæus, the Ulaï of Daniel, where he saw in vision the ram with two horns, and the goat which "came from the west on the face of the whole earth, and touched not the ground." This stream originally passed through Susa, and its ancient bed may still be traced. Here are the ruins of the mighty citadel where so many valiant heroes fought, and the magnificent palace where were displayed so much pride, wealth, luxury, cruelty, and sensuality. Now there are no inhabitants. Lions roar around its palaces; wolves, lynxes, foxes, and jackals prowl amid its ruins; wild boars and porcupines range the silentness of its approaches, and francolins and partridges find shelter in the deepness of its surrounding coverts.

The burial-place of the prophet Daniel is acknowledged by Jews, Sabæans, and Mohammedans to be at Shushan. The consecrated spot is visited by many pious pilgrims, who come to offer up prayers and to bury their dead in the holy ground. Many traditions are current concerning the great prophet.

Benjamin of Tudela, A. D. 1160–1173, states that Shushan then contained "very large and handsome buildings of ancient date. It has seven thousand Jewish inhabitants, with fourteen synagogues, in front of one of which is the sepulcher of Daniel, who rests in peace. The river Ulai divides the city into two parts, which are connected by a bridge; that portion of it which is inhabited by the Jews contains markets, to which all trade is confined, and there all the rich dwell; on the other side of the river they are poor, because they are deprived of the above-mentioned advantages, and have even no gardens or orchards. These circumstances gave rise to jealousy, which was fostered by the belief that all honor and riches originated in the possession of the remains of the prophet Daniel, who rests in peace, and who was buried on the favored side of the river. A request was made by the poor for permission to remove the sepulcher to the other side, but it was rejected; upon which a war arose, and was carried on between the two parties for a length of time. This strife lasted until 'their souls became loath,' and they came to a mutual agreement, by which it was arranged that the coffin which contained Daniel's bones should be deposited alternately every year on either side. Both parties faithfully adhered to this arrangement, until it was interrupted by the interference of Sanjar Sháh-ben-Sháh, who governs Persia, and holds supreme power over forty-nine of its kings. . . . When this great emperor Sanjar, king of Persia, came to Shushan, and saw that the coffin of Daniel was removed from one side to the other, he crossed the bridge with a very numerous retinue, accompanied by Jews and Mohammedans, and inquired into the reason of these proceedings. Upon being told what we have now related, he declared it to be derogatory to the honor of Daniel, and commanded that the distance between the two banks should be exactly measured, that Daniel's coffin should be deposited in another coffin made of glass, and that it should be suspended from the center of the bridge by chains of iron. A place of worship was erected on the spot, open to every one who desires to say his prayers, whether he be Jew or Gentile: and the coffin of Daniel is suspended from the bridge unto this very day. The king commanded that, in honor of Daniel, nobody should be allowed to fish in the river one mile on each side of the coffin."

Other similar traditions are current. The tomb of Daniel, in which, however, his remains do not, in all probability, rest, is a resort not only for pilgrims who lodge there at night, but also for robbers who make it the rendezvous for their plundering expeditions.*

The palace at Susa, at the summit of the great platform, fronting a little west of north, and commanding a magnificent view over the Susanian plains to the mountains of Lúristán, was exhumed by Mr. Loftus and General Williams. It proved to have been almost an exact duplicate of the Chehl Minar of Persepolis. It consisted of several magnificent groups of columns having a frontage of three hundred and forty-three feet nine inches, and a depth of two hundred and forty-four feet. The central phalanx

* Loftus, *Chaldea and Susiana*, p. 317, *et seq.*

contained thirty-six columns in six rows. Sixty-four feet two inches from this phalanx, on the west, north, and east, were an equal number of columns arranged in double rows of six each. The capitals of the fluted pillars in the eastern colonnade were two half-griffins looking in opposite directions. Those of the western colonnade were two half-bulls, while those of the northern colonnade and central phalanx were lotus buds, with pendent leaves, volutes, and two half-bulls. The bases of the pillars of the porticoes were bell-shaped, and ornamented with double or triple rows of lotus, while the bases of the central pillar were square. The central pillar cluster and the three porches were separately roofed. Beams stretched from pillar to pillar supported roof and entablature. There were no walls, but the great palace was open to all the winds of heaven. Such appear to have been the main features of the palace.

"Nothing could be more appropriate than this method at Susa and Persepolis, the spring residences of the Persian monarchs. It must be considered that these columnar halls were the equivalents of the modern throne-rooms, that here all public business was dispatched, and that here the king might sit and enjoy the beauties of the landscape. With the rich plains of Susa and Persepolis before him, he could well, after his winter's residence at Babylon, dispense with massive walls, which would only check the warm, fragrant breeze from those verdant prairies adorned with the choicest flowers. A massive roof, covering the whole expanse of columns, would be too cold and dismal, whereas curtains around the central group would serve to admit both light and warmth. Nothing can be conceived better adapted to the climate or the season." *

"Such edifices as the Chehl Minar at Persepolis, and its duplicate at Susa—where long vistas of columns met the eye on every side, and the great central cluster was supported by lighter detached groups, combining similarity of form with some variety of ornament, where richly colored drapings contrasted with the cool gray stone of the building, and a golden roof overhung a pavement of many hues—must have been handsome, from whatever side they were contemplated, and for general richness and harmony of effect may have compared favorably with any edifices which, up to the time of their construction, had been erected in any country or by any people." †

To complete the picture of this palace, other ruins, especially those at Persepolis, must be studied. The great palace was situated on a terraced platform "composed of solid masses of hewn stone which were united by metal clamps, probably of iron or lead." This platform is ascended by broad stair-

* Loftus, *Chaldea and Susiana*, p. 375.
† Rawlinson, *Ancient Monarchies*, vol. iii, p. 328.

ways elaborately ornamented with mythologic figures of lions devouring bulls, guardsmen, rows of cypress-trees, rosettes, processions of the nations bringing tribute to the great king, attendants carrying articles for the table or the toilet, and inscriptions commemorating his own glorious deeds or those of his ancestors, and recognizing the gods to whom they owed their conquests and glory.

On this broad elevated platform were the palaces, for there were several at Persepolis, and probably at the other capitals. The massive walls, the spacious rooms, the reception halls, the throne-room, the guard rooms, the stair-ways, the pillars and colonnades, the bases and capitals, the porticoes and chambers, the entablatures and inscriptions, the sculptures and ornamentations, the furnishment and garnishment, the throne itself, the plating of gold, the beautiful hangings of purple, the display, and magnificence, and glory, and power, and wealth—in all this the palace of Susa far outdoes the palaces of modern times.

The royal palace was furnished with a magnificence commensurate with the wealth and pride of the king. The floors were paved with precious stones of blue, white, black, and red, so arranged as to form beautiful patterns. Richest carpeting was placed here and there so as to add to the appearance of comfort and luxury. Magnificent hangings of white, green, and violet, fastened with fine linen and purple cords to silver rings, stretched from pillar of marble to pillar of marble, screening the guests, and at the same time ad-

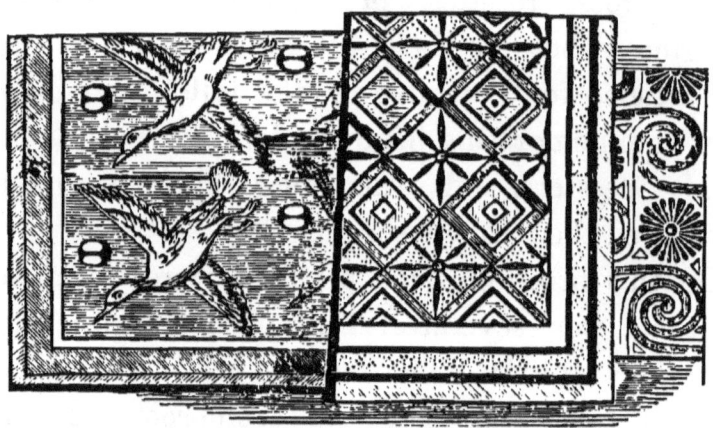

TESSELLATED PAVEMENTS.

mitting the cool breezes of summer. The ceilings of the rooms were covered with plates of gold.

Four pillars of gold, inlaid with precious stones, supported an embroidered canopy with inwrought mythologic figures of bulls and lions and other objects, under which stood the golden throne of the king. Couches resplendent with silver and gold filled the rooms, on which guests reclined at ease. Over the royal bed in the private chamber of the monarch was the golden vine with the grapes imitated by stones of priceless value. It was the work of Theodore the Samian, and the gift of Pythius, a rich Lydian, to Darius. A golden plane-tree, also the gift of Pythius, was the companion of the vine. Here, too, was the celebrated bowl of solid gold.

All were rare works of the highest metallurgical art.

The throne was of silver and gold. It was an elevated chair, without arms, but with a high back, cushioned and ornamented with a fringe. Along the back and legs were carvings or moldings which exhibited little artistic skill. The legs terminated in lions' feet resting on fluted hemispheres. The sides of the chair below the seat were paneled and plain.

The feet of the monarch rested on a footstool the legs of which terminated in bulls' feet. Perhaps originally a religious meaning attached to this symbolism. Winged human-headed bulls and lions of large size guarded the entrances to Assyrian palaces. On the portal was a figure strangling a lion. The winged bull symbolized Ninip, the Chaldean Hercules, perhaps also represented in the figure strangling the lion. He was "the crusher of opponents, he who rolls along the mass of heaven and earth, treader of the wide earth, head of nations, bestower of scepters, Lord of lords, the deity who changes not his purposes, the light of heaven and earth, the hero of the gods, lord over the face of the whirlwind, son of El, the Sublime."

Nergal was symbolized by the winged human-headed lion. He was "the god of arms and bows, the great hero, king of fight, master of battles, champion of the gods, god of the chase." These gigantic figures may have had a talismanic value. The Cuthæans, according to the Bible, worshiped Nergal. The natural lion was more frequently used as a symbol of Nergal than the winged lion. These two, then, Ninip and Nergal, the gods of war and of the chase, were the foundation of the Persian throne; or they remained as survivals of Chaldean and Assyrian symbolism.

The ancient Lydians used the same symbolism. The molten sea of the Hebrews was supported by "twelve oxen," "and on the borders that were between the ledges were lions, oxen, and cherubims." Solomon made a throne of ivory overlaid with "best gold;" "two lions stood beside the stays. And twelve lions stood there on the one side and the other upon the six steps." The palace of the Parthian city Hatra had upon its south side eight human-headed bulls. The north side is so much in ruins that the character of its ornamentation cannot be determined.

The kings of Parthia, probably, imitated the Persian kings in the magnificence of their palaces, though they must have fallen far behind in the wealth of display. Philostratus says of the royal palace of Babylon: "The palace is roofed with brass, and a bright light flashes from it. It has chambers for the women, and chambers for the men, and porticoes, partly glittering with silver, partly with cloth-of-gold embroideries, partly with solid slabs of gold, let into the walls, like pictures. The subjects of these embroideries are taken from the Greek mythology, and include representations of Andromeda, Amymoné, and of Orpheus, who is frequently repeated. . . . Datis is, moreover, represented, destroying Naxos with his fleet, and Artaphernes besieging Eretria, and Xerxes gaining his famous victories. You behold the occupation of Athens, and the battle of Thermopylæ, and other points still more characteristic of the great Persian war, rivers drunk up and disappearing from the face of the earth, and a bridge stretched across the sea, and a canal cut through Athos. . . . One chamber for the men has a roof fashioned into a vault like the heaven, composed entirely of sapphires, which are the bluest of stones, and resemble the sky in color. Golden images of the gods whom they worship are set up about the vault, and show like stars in the firmament. This is the chamber in which the king delivers his judgments. Four golden magic-wheels hang from its roof, and threaten the monarch with the Divine Nemesis, if he exalts himself above the condition of man. These wheels are called 'the tongues of the gods,' and are set in their places by the magi who frequent the palace."

Polybius says that the whole wood-work of the palace at Ecbatana was covered with plates of gold or silver, and that the building was roofed with silver tiles. The temple of Anaitis was in the same mannor richly adorned.* After the successive plunderings of Darius, Alexander, and Seleucus Nicator, the tiles and plating of the palace at Ecbatana brought to Antiochus the Great nearly five millions of dollars.†

This capital city is called "Shushan" seven times, and "the city Shushan" twice, in the Book of Esther. The expression "Shushan the palace" occurs ten times. The latter was the royal quarter, and contained palaces, gardens, areas, residences of the officers of the court with their families and servants, temples, and various dependent buildings. The whole area was encompassed by a strong wall, and protected by towers and the lofty Acropolis at the western angle.

"This was Shushan the castle, the upper town, the royal quarter—'Shushan the palace' of the A. V. Here Daniel dwelt (Dan. viii, 2), and at the western foot of the Acropolis on the bank of the Shapur is his traditional grave. Here Nehemiah also found a temporary residence. Neh. i, 1. When 'the great king' sojourned at Shushan, doubtless many thousand people dwelt within this space, just as during the feasts at Jerusalem prodigious multitudes, living as Orientals can, were able to find room in the holy city. Ctesias tells us ‡ that the king of Persia furnished provisions daily for twenty-five thousand men,

---

* Polybius, x; xxvii, 10–12. † Herodotus, i, 98, note.
‡ Barnes upon Dan. v, 1.

all of whom we presume were never at one time resident in the upper city." *

The site of "Shushan the palace" is probably the whole diamond-shaped area on the east of the Shapur, with its acute angles fronting north and south, and marked by three mounds. In the northern angle is the palace mound, some four thousand feet in circumference. Here was the palace which we have described. Trilingual inscriptions found upon pedestals ascribe its erection to Darius Hystaspis. Like the famous Hall of Xerxes at Persepolis, the Chehl Minar, this was doubtless a Hall of State as distinguished from the royal residence. It seems also to have been used for religious purposes, for it is called a temple in the inscriptions upon the pedestals, and contained effigies of the gods.† Darius is represented upon the sculptures at Persepolis as a pontiff king.

In the western angle of the diamond is the citadel mound, the loftiest of all, two thousand eight hundred and fifty feet in circuit at the summit. Occupying the whole south-eastern side of the diamond is "the great platform," reaching an elevation of from forty to seventy feet. Each side is about three thousand feet in length and the area about sixty acres. This diamond-shaped series of mounds includes above one hundred acres. This is "Shushan the palace"

* *The Lowell Hebrew Club, The Book of Esther*, p. 99.
† Loftus, *Chaldea and Susiana*, pp. 371, 372.

as distinguished from "the city Shushan." It was, doubtless, the strong-hold of the city.

The position and architectural character of the Hall of State have been determined, but we know little of the other buildings of this royal quarter except by inference from discoveries at other capitals. Among other buildings there must have been a royal palace, and to this palace we must transfer so much of description as evidently belongs to a domiciliary residence. Such descriptions have been applied to the single building which has been unearthed, but certainly without reason.

Strabo says: "The following mentioned by Polycletus are perhaps customary practices: At Susa each king builds in the citadel, as memorials of the administration of his government, a dwelling for himself, treasure-houses, and magazines for tribute collected (in kind)." * Xerxes had a royal palace at Persepolis, and probably at Susa.

The Hall of State—the *bēthän*—seems to be mentioned but twice in the story of Esther. The great feast was held in the court of the garden of this hall. The queen's palace, where she entertained the king and Haman was probably south-east of this hall and separated from it by a garden. Esther i, 5; vii, 7, 8. The king's palace—the *bayith*—was a separate building. So likewise the first house of the women and

* Strabo, vol. iii, p. 139.

the second house of the women. These several buildings with their courts and gardens were closely connected, and probably all situated in the northern angle of the diamond. Their exact location is conjectural. The main entrance to this seraglio department of "Shushan the palace"—Shushan the *bērăh*—was a gate which was in front and at some distance from the Hall of State. At Persepolis, and doubtless here also, the propylon "consisted of a square hall inclosing a group of four pillars." The gate was through this hall, or more probably by its side. At this gate a court was held. Guards and servants were there, and it was perhaps the only public entrance to the seraglio quarter. There may have been another gate on the east in connection with the king's palace, which may be located provisionally in the north-east corner of this palace mound. If so, this second may be "the king's gate." Midway between the king's palace and the Hall of State we may locate the queen's palace, west of which was the second house of the women, and between the last and the king's palace the first house of the women.

III.

THE BANQUET OF WINE.

"The king made a feast."—ESTHER i, 5.
"The heart of the king was merry with wine."—ESTHER i, 10.

ORIENTAL nations are noted for the hospitality of the people. Abraham made an impromptu feast for the "three men" who tarried with him when on their journey to Sodom. Guests were received and dismissed with goodly viands, and departed "with mirth, and with songs, and with tabret, and with harp."

A feast graced seasons of domestic joy. Birthdays and marriages were celebrated with special brilliancy. At sheep-shearing the guests often became "merry with wine." Sacrifices to the gods were accompanied with gladsome feasts. There were vintage feasts, and the solemnity of the funeral was relieved by feasting. Every three years, among the Hebrews, there were charitable feasts, to which they invited the Levite, the stranger, the fatherless, and the widow. The rich vied with each other in the brilliancy of their entertainments, and freely poured out their wealth to procure the rarest viands and the products of the highest culinary art. Kings impoverished their subjects that they might feast their favorites and noble guests sumptuously. In luxurious living the later Persians rivaled all other peoples.

When Darius Codomannus went out with his mighty army to meet Alexander the Great at Issus he was accompanied with his whole family, harem, and court, and all the paraphernalia of wealth, luxury, and splendor. In his immense baggage train were six hundred mules and three hundred camels laden with gold and silver. When the conqueror took Persepolis it required five thousand camels and an immense number of mules to convey the royal treasures of the Persian king to Susa and Ecbatana.

When Cyrus wished to persuade the Persians to revolt he invited them to an assembly, and commanded them to bring their reaping-hooks. Herodotus relates: "When, in obedience to the orders which they had received, the Persians came with their reaping-hooks, Cyrus led them to a tract of ground, about eighteen or twenty furlongs each way, covered with thorns, and ordered them to clear it before the day was out. They accomplished their task, upon which he issued a second order to them, to take the bath the day following and again come to him. Meantime he collected together all his father's flocks, both sheep and goats, and all his oxen, and slaughtered them, and made ready to give an entertainment to the entire Persian army. Wine, too, and bread of the choicest kinds were prepared for the occasion.

When the morrow came and the Persians appeared, he bade them recline upon the grass and enjoy themselves. After the feast was over he requested them to tell him 'which they liked best, to-day's work or yesterday's?' They answered that 'the contrast was indeed strong: yesterday brought them nothing but what was bad, to-day every thing that was good.' Cyrus instantly seized on their reply, and laid bare his purpose in these words: 'Ye men of Persia, thus do matters stand with you. If you choose to hearken to my words, you may enjoy these and ten thousand similiar delights, and never condescend to any slavish toil; but if you will not hearken, prepare yourselves for unnumbered toils as hard as yesterday's. Now, therefore, follow my bidding and be free.'"* Thus Cyrus feasted the whole Persian army and persuaded them to strike for freedom from Median rule.

In Judith we read of a great feast appointed by Nebuchadnezzar after a signal victory, at which his whole army was royally entertained during one hundred and twenty days (Judith i, 16). Belshazzar feasted a thousand lords, and Alexander ten thousand men.

Usually the king of Persia dined alone, and only on special occasions was he served with his guests. Sometimes he admitted the queen, the queen-mother, and one or two children—less frequently even his

---
* Herodotus, i, 126.

THE BANQUET OF WINE.

brothers. At a "banquet of wine" his intimate companions were privileged guests. The king reclined at the feast on a golden-footed couch and drank the wine of Helbon, while his guests, seated on the floor, were less nobly served. At the great banquets the less distinguished of the company were entertained in the outer court, accessible to the public, while the more distinguished were admitted to the king's private apartments and feasted in the chamber opposite the king's chamber, from which they were separated by a curtain. On certain great occasions the king threw off his reserve and presided openly at the banquet, talking and drinking with all, and making merry with his friends, who reclined on couches of silver and gold, and drank "royal wine" from golden cups. Oriental rules of courtesy and the personal will of the monarch were the law at these feasts.

The king himself had the choicest luxuries, which he did not often share with the multitude. The wheat of Assos, the wine of Helbon, water from distant streams, salt from the oasis of Ammon, and every thing rarest and best, were for his table.

PERSIAN KING.

The delicacies of the empire were at his command.

His amusements were few, and not especially ennobling. He played at dice with his near relatives. The wager was sometimes very heavy—thousands of gold and valuable slaves. He amused himself by carving in wood. His most noble sport was hunting the lion and the wild boar, but sometimes he stooped to pursue less noble beasts of the chase.

According to Rawlinson: "At the present day, among the *bons vivants* of Persia, it is usual to sit for hours before dinner drinking wine and eating dried fruits, such as filberts, almonds, pistachio nuts, melon-seeds, etc. A party, indeed, often sits down at seven o'clock and the dinner is not brought in till eleven. The dessert dishes, intermingled as they are with highly seasoned delicacies, are supposed to have the effect of stimulating the appetite, but, in reality, the solid dishes, which are served up at the end of the feast, are rarely tasted. The passion, too, for wine-drinking is as marked among the Persians of the present day, notwithstanding the prohibitions of the Prophet, as it was in the time of Herodotus. It is quite appalling, indeed, to see the quantity of liquor which some of these topers habitually consume, and they usually prefer spirits to wine." Herodotus says: "It is also their general practice to deliberate upon affairs of weight when they are drunk; and then on the morrow, when they are sober, the decision to which they came the night before is put before them by the master of the house in which it was made;

and if it is then approved they act on it; if not, they set it aside. Sometimes, however, they are sober at their first deliberation, but in this case they always reconsider the matter under the influence of wine." According to Tacitus, who seems to approve the custom, the Germans had a similar practice, and Plato says that it prevailed among the Thracians, the Scythians, the Celts, the Iberians, and the Carthaginians. Daris of Samos says that at the feast of Mithras, held once a year, the king was bound to get drunk.*

Xerxes was ever fond of display. He gave rich presents to a beautiful plane-tree; he caused to be erected a throne of white marble upon which to sit while reviewing his army; the spears of the soldiers who were near his presence were adorned with gold and silver apples and pomegranates; and every thing was on a scale of the greatest splendor. The following circumstance is related. The war-tent of Xerxes was left with Mardonius in Greece, and fell into the hands of the enemy. "When Pausanius, therefore, saw the tent with its adornments of gold and silver, and its hangings of divers colors, he gave commandment to the bakers and the cooks to make him ready a banquet in such fashion as was their wont for Mardonius. Then they made ready as they were bidden, and Pausanius, beholding the couches of gold and silver daintily decked out with their rich covertures,

* Herodotus, i, 133.

and the tables of gold and silver laid, and the feast itself prepared with all magnificence, was astonished at the good things which were set before him, and, being in a pleasant mood, gave commandment to his own followers to make ready a Spartan supper. When the suppers were both served, and it was apparent how vast a difference lay between the two, Pausanius laughed and sent his servants to call to him the Greek generals. On their coming he pointed to the two boards and said: 'I sent for you, O Greeks, to show you the folly of this Median captain, who, when he enjoyed such fare as this, must needs come here to rob us of our penury.'" *

The great king had returned from his successful campaign in Egypt. His influential friends urged other and greater conquests. He could extend his dominion to the west and annex Greece to the vast empire he inherited from his father. He called an assembly to deliberate upon his gigantic scheme. He could take an inventory of his possessions, listen to reports from distant provinces, discuss plans, raise an army and gather munitions of war, and be ready to take the field. He could impress subject princes with his own glorious majesty, exhibit his royal power, display the magnificence of his court, lavish his wealth in the regal splendor of such an entertainment as the world had never seen, and bind powerful friends to

* Herodotus, ix, 82.

his interests by the distribution of kingly presents. Princes, nobles, warriors, and statesmen came from a hundred and seven and twenty provinces, from India even unto Ethiopia. The *élite* of the army were there; the nobles, the magnates, and the grandees of the kingdom were present, "when he showed the riches of his glorious kingdom and the honor of his excellent majesty many days, *even* an hundred and four-score days." After this there was a still more royal feast of seven days given to all the people that were present in "Shushan the palace."

This was the celebrated assembly which discussed the question of the invasion of Greece. At first the king was disposed to follow the advice of Mardonius, who favored the expedition, but upon consideration he yielded to the more sober reasoning of Artabanus, who feared the consequences of an invasion of Europe. Afterward, when they had been deliberating "many days," Xerxes was led to change his mind by a vision which stood over him every night. Then, by his command, Artabanus, clad in the king's garments, took his seat upon the royal throne, and then lay down to sleep upon the royal bed, to see whether the same vision would make him a visit. As he fell asleep the same dream appeared to him as had troubled the rest of the king, and addressed him in words of stern rebuke and threatening. "In such words, as Artabanus thought, the vision threatened him, and then endeavored to burn out his eyes with red-hot irons. At this he shrieked, and, leaping from his couch, hurried to Xerxes, and sitting down at his side, gave him a full account of the vision." Henceforth active preparations were made for the expedition.

"This counterfeit phantom frightens Xerxes out of the conclusion of his second thought and his better judgment, and overcomes the maturer wisdom of Artabanus, his uncle. It is this, in fact, that seems to turn the scale, and settle the point that the great expedition shall be undertaken. Superstition is potent in its way; but that a phantom should have assailed a man of the courage and wisdom of Artabanus with hot irons, and alarmed him with the attempt to burn out his eyes, and actually have succeeded in driving him, with a loud outcry, from his couch and his room, and been regarded by him still without question as a veritable apparition, is strongly suggestive of a brain from which the fumes of the wine-cup have not wholly passed away." *

This banquet at Susa was doubtless given in the early spring of B. C. 483—there were thrones of the kingdom also at Ecbatana, Persepolis, and Babylon, where the court was sometimes held—and was a true *symposium*, or drinking feast. After keeping open house for six months, he appointed the crowning

* Herod., vii, 8-19; Lowell Hebrew Club, *The Book of Esther*, p. 20.

feast of seven days "in the court of the garden of the King's palace," the paradise, or garden, connected with the Hall of State.

The king himself, a man remarkable for his natural beauty, was the cynosure of all eyes. The whole dress was such as to give grace and dignity to the person. The robe, or "Median garment," was of royal purple, and probably of richest silk and embroidered with gold. It was close-fitting at the neck and chest, with loose, open sleeves, and with ample long-flowing folds extending below the ankles and confined about the waist with a girdle. The tunic, or under-garment, reached from the neck to the knee and covered the arms tightly to the wrists. It was purple mixed with white — royal colors — and of rich material. The trousers were of crimson, and the long tapering shoes of deep yellow or saffron, buttoned in front and reaching high in the instep. The distinguishing feature of the dress of the king, by which it specially differed from that of the nobles, was the peculiar head-dress. It was "a tall stiff cap, slightly swelling as it ascended, flat at top and terminating in a ring or circle which projected beyond the lines of the sides. Round it, probably near the bottom, was worn a fillet or band—the *diadem* proper—which was blue, spotted with white." Such a head-dress would readily distinguish the king from the members of his court. They wore simple fillets, or comparatively low caps. The other garments of the king, already described, though of richer material and somewhat different in color, yet closely resembled the dress of the nobles.

The monarch was further distinguished by the golden scepter which, in the representations which have been discovered, is frequently seen in the king's hand. It was a simple rod five feet long, ornamented by a ball at the top and tapering nearly to a point at the bottom. The king held it in his right hand near the thick end; the thin end, whether he sat or walked, he rested on the ground in front of him, the scepter sloping to the ground.

The use of the parasol was also confined to the king. It had a long thick stem terminated by a

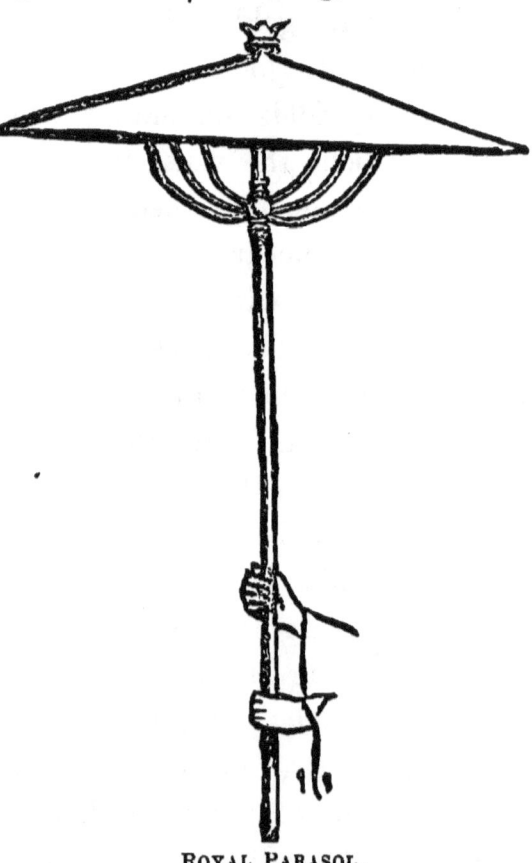

ROYAL PARASOL.

peculiar ornament at the top. The shade was tent-like in shape and without curtain or tassel. It was kept open by curved supports, and on great occasions was held over the king's head by an attendant who walked behind.

On all state occasions, when the king received embassadors, royal or noble visitors, and high officers of the court, when he received reports from secretaries or governors of provinces or military leaders, when he issued commands or royal edicts, the diadem was upon his brow, the golden scepter in his hand, and the royal parasol over his head.

KING WITH ATTENDANTS.

The king wore golden earrings, often set with precious jewels, bejeweled golden bracelets, and a twisted golden collar. In his girdle he carried a short sword, the sheath of which was formed of a single precious stone, jasper, agate, or lapis lazuli.

FAN, OR FLY-CHASER.

The parasol-bearer and the fan-bearer, who also carried "the royal pocket-handkerchief," were always near the king. "The fan, or fly-chaser, had a long straight handle ornamented with a sort of beading, which held a brush of some springy fibrous matter. The bearer, whose place was directly behind the monarch, held his implement, which bent forward gracefully, nearly at arm's-length over the master's head." Sometimes the fan-bearer held in his hand a bottle of perfumery. This was probably placed in the water wherewith the king and his guests washed before meals.

SCENT-BOTTLE.

The Persians made great use of perfumeries. When the royal tiara was not in use, it was laid away with a mixture of myrrh and labyzus. The Persians were supposed to have been the inventors of aromatic unguents. To give himself a beautiful complexion, the king, according to Pliny, anointed his person with an unguent composed of lion's fat, palm wine, saffron, and helianthus. At Arbela, Alexander found among the camp equipage of Darius a case of unguents. The "royal ointment" of the Parthian kings was composed of cinnamon, spikenard, myrrh, cassia, gum styrax, saffron, cardamom, wine, honey, and sixteen other ingredients.

The tribute of frankincense from Arabia was a thousand talents' weight annually, much of which was doubtless required by the royal court. As was the case in Egypt and Greece, so in Persia, unguent vases were of choicest alabaster.

There were many other officers of the court less closely attached to the person of the king—the steward of the household, the master of the horse, the chief eunuch, who had charge of the harem; spies, who kept the king informed concerning all that transpired about the court and in the kingdom, and hence called his "eyes and ears;" secretaries, who wrote the king's letters, edicts, and books of records; messengers; ushers, who introduced with becoming formalities strangers to the king; "tasters," who tried all the food placed before him to guard against poison; cup-bearers, who poured out his wine; chamberlains, who assisted him to retire; and musicians, who amused him with harp and song. There were also multitudes of guards, door-keepers, huntsmen, grooms, cooks, and various domestic servants. And then we must add visitors and guests, princes and nobles, captives and foreign refugees, hostages, embassadors, and travelers. Indeed, we are informed that the king fed daily at his palace fifteen thousand persons, at a cost of four hundred talents. A thousand beasts were slaughtered for each meal, besides poultry, ostriches, and other birds. These estimates, however, may refer to special feasts, and not to the ordinary repasts. The great feast would require an unusually large number of attendants.

"Solomon's provision for one day was thirty measures of fine flour, and three-score measures of meal, ten fat oxen, and twenty oxen out of the pastures, and a hundred sheep, beside harts, and roebucks, and fallow-deer, and fatted fowl." 1 Kings iv, 22, 23.

Perhaps there were none of the poorer class present at this banquet. The ordinary dress of the poorer class was the tunic and trousers, a felt cap or a mere linen or muslin rag for the head, a strap about the waist, and high shoes upon the feet. The richer class of Persia adopted much of the costume of the court— flowing robes, embroidered tiaras, also drawers, shirts, socks, and gloves. They wore collars and bracelets of gold, while the sheaths and handles of their swords and daggers were also of gold, perhaps adorned with gems. The trappings of their horses were of the richest character, the bit being often of solid gold. Their tables were inlaid with silver and gold; they had gorgeous couches, soft carpets, and gold and silver plate.

In their early history the Persians were temperate in eating and drinking. Wheaten bread, barley cakes, meat, and water satisfied them, and they had but one meal each day. The poorer class subsisted largely upon the natural fruits of the soil. Luxury and self-indulgence came in later. Wine became the common beverage, and they prided themselves on the amount they could drink.

The usual rules of court etiquette were largely adopted among the people, and they enjoyed the same liberty with respect to wives, concubines, and eunuchs. The education of their sons consisted in those manly exercises by which they would be prepared for war, and certain moral teachings drawn from standard legendary poems. They cared naught for trade and commerce, and labor was for slaves. With the advance of luxury, they curled their hair and beards, or even wore false hair, beards, and mustachios. Cosmetics beautified the complexion, and coloring matter on the eyelids increased the apparent size and brilliancy of their eyes. And there came absolute rule, tyranny, barbarity, a blunted moral sense, horrible punishments, treachery, brutality, and nameless crimes.

The Hall of State, the royal palace, the many buildings of the northern angle of the diamond, and their surrounding paradises, were the scene of all the beauty, pride, wealth, luxury, and glory of the great empire of kingdoms. Emeralds were gathered from Egypt, Media, and Cyprus; green rubies from Bactria, and red rubies and carbuncles from Caria; opals and sapphires from Cyprus, and opals also from Egypt and Asia Minor; amethysts from Cyprus, Egypt, Galatia, and Armenia, and sards from Babylonia; jaspers from Cyprus, Asia Minor, and Persia proper, and the lapis lazuli from Egypt, Cyprus, and Media; agates from Carmania, Susiana, and Armenia, and the topaz from Upper Egypt; jets from Lycia, and garnets and beryls from Armenia. These were wrought into most precious jewelry and blazed on the breasts of Persian beauties. They adorned bracelets, armlets, chains for the neck, and sheaths for swords. Pearls from the ocean lent themselves to assist in this display of wealth, beauty, and magnificence. The floors were mosaics of valuable stones. The tables were gold and silver and set with gems. Vases of agate filled with skillfully prepared perfumes steeped the air in fragrance. Flowers of rich colors and sweet aroma smiled in their more modest, winning beauty. The mountains and deserts of Thibet and India were swept for their gold. Rivers of Lydia gave up their wealth. The mines of Kerman, Armenia, Asia Minor, and the Elburz brought their silver. Damascus sent the most valuable marble. Phenicia sent her purple, and Babylonia her embroideries rich in their revelations of mythologic lore. The rich carpets came from the looms of Babylon and Sardis; the splendid shawls from Kashmir and India; the fine linen from Borsippa and Egypt; the coverlets from Damascus; the muslins from Babylonia; and the noble cedar from Lebanon.

So splendid are the preparations that guest after guest, as they arrive, can but exclaim in astonishment and wonder: "White and violet awnings, fastened with cords of fine linen and purple to rings of silver and pillars of white marble; couches of gold and silver on a pavement of blue stone, and white marble, and alabaster, and red stone! And they gave drink in vessels of gold, even vessels differing from one another; and royal wine was abundant, according to the hand of the king." Esther i, 6, 7. Strabo says of the Persians: "Their couches, drinking-cups, and other articles are so brilliantly ornamented that they gleam with gold and silver." *

The stones for these columns and pavements must have been brought from a great distance. As specimens of the mineral relics of Shushan, Loftus mentions white marble, red sandstone, Oriental alabaster, polished basalt, blue limestone, and yellow limestone.†

The king, crowned with the diadem of empire, clad in richest attire, numerously attended, proud and selfish, scepter in hand, "sat on the throne of his kingdom," as he sat to view the battles of Thermopylæ and Salamis, and "showed the riches of his glorious kingdom and the honor of his excellent majesty." Nobles and princes from the one hundred and twenty-seven provinces, in Median garments, graced the occasion by their presence. The feast was the grandest held by Xerxes during his reign. It lasted one hundred and eighty days, and culminated in a special seven-days' feast of unexampled magnificence.

* Strabo, vol. iii, p. 139.
† Loftus, *Chaldea and Susiana*, pp. 346, 376, 404, 408, 409, 415.

The king drank the wine of Helbon. His guests received "royal wine in abundance," poured into golden goblets from silver decanters. Nuts gathered from many forests were served in dishes of agate and onyx. Luscious tropical fruits, inviting to the palate, were displayed on golden and silver plates. Figs, dates, sweetmeats, and all delicacies were passed again and again. All grains, fowl of every wing, flesh of many kinds of beasts, all foods of the soil—these prepared in the highest style of culinary art, the praise of the epicure—were served in many courses.

Servants hasten to and fro to do their master's bidding. The voice of song is heard. The shout of laughter echoes through the halls and gardens. There is many a sally of wit. And still flows the royal wine. Guests come from distant provinces and return. Suns rise and set. Weeks and months pass. There are the same hurry and excitement and prodigality and courtesies and compliments and beauty and pride and revelry and boasting of "excellent majesty." Outside the palace, throughout the vast empire, there are thousands of men, women, and children starving for want of bread. What cares the king? Men, women, and children are of no value, except as they administer to his personal enjoyment. And so the feast continues and, as ever, the royal wine flows. Garlands delicately woven by skillful fingers crown those who are mighty to drink wine. Festoons of many flowers and evergreens arch the broad entrances, entwine the pillars, and leap from colonnade to colonnade. At night lights from Oriental chandeliers, shining upon tables and ceilings of gold, seem to start up ten thousand fires, and to make every pearl and gem and chain and cup and plate of gold a blazing star. The eye is wearied and almost blinded by the dazzling splendors and blazing beauty.

But affairs of state must occupy some portion of the time of the king and his counselors. They consult concerning the glory of the kingdom, and especially concerning the conquest of Greece, upon which the king is about to enter. They talk of the great Cambyses and the greater Cyrus, and the conversation seems to inspire the king with the determination to excel them all in the glory of his majesty. He will raise an army such as the world has never seen, and conquer Europe and annex it to the empire. He receives reports from all the provinces, issues edicts, and makes requisitions for troops, ships, gold, and supplies. He punishes criminals and pardons offenders. He raises some to positions of honor and reduces others to poverty. He gives rich presents and grants important privileges to his favorites, and disgraces those who offend him and banishes them from the kingdom. There are, probably, impressive religious services. The magi are invoked to decide important questions, either by lot or by means of magical rites.

There are, doubtless, many military reviews to feed the excitement of the multitude. The king plays at dice with noble guests for immense stakes. There are royal hunting expeditions in the forests or in some of the king's paradises.

There are trophies of victories and memorials of conquests. The king's word is law. A world lies at his feet, and he stands upon the necks of princes. Wealth is poured into his treasury, tributes and gifts from all the provinces. Like Solomon when visited by the Queen of Sheba, he shows all his treasures—the palaces, his throne, his gold and silver plate, his royal jewelry, his uncounted wealth, his trophies of war and conquest, his eunuchs, his slaves, his noble captives and hostages, and his royal inscriptions. No other monarch has ever ruled over so broad an empire, and no other has received so rich a tribute, or the homage of so many kings "from India even unto Ethiopia."

Still flows wine from the royal cellars. None is compelled to drink more than he wishes. The Greeks at their feasts had a *symposiarch*, the Romans an *arbiter bibendi*, the Jews a master of the feast. The drinking was under the direction of the master, who received his orders from the throne. Not so here, but each guest drinks to suit his pleasure. This is provided in a special edict of the king—" No compelling." "The wine of the kingdom" flows abundantly. Nobles become drunken. Eyes are red, steps unsteady, hands tremble, the tongue is loosened, and pride is fed.

The "hundred and four-score days" have already passed, and the king has made "a feast unto all the people that are present in Shushan the palace, both unto great and small, seven days, in the court of the garden of the king's palace." The king, inflamed with wine, boasts of the strength of his good right arm, his personal prowess, his bravery in battle, his military renown, the homage and loyalty of his subjects, the multitude of his slaves, and the beauty of his queen. And still he drinks the wine of Helbon. The guests vie with each other in feeding his vanity, and praise him in unmeasured terms of flattery. The climax is reached when the king declares that the nobles and princes and guests must themselves see Queen Vashti in order to fully appreciate his happiness in her possession. They applaud his suggestion.

Meantime Vashti has been feasting the women in " the royal house." It is the seventh day, the last day of the feast. That the beautiful queen may be ushered into his presence in a manner befitting her dignity and position, he commands the seven chamberlains, or eunuchs—Mehuman, Biztha, Harbona, Bigtha, Abagtha, Zethar, and Carcas—" to bring Vashti the queen before the king with the crown royal, to show the people and the princes her beauty, for she was fair to look on."

This is not the only case in which an Oriental monarch has wished to have his own estimate of his queen's loveliness confirmed by the opinion of other judges of female beauty. Herodotus gives an account of the assassination of Candaules, king of Sardis: "Now it happened that this Candaules was in love with his own wife, and not only so, but thought her the fairest woman in the whole world. This fancy had strange consequences. There was in his body-guard a man whom he specially favored, Gyges, the son of Dascylus. All affairs of great moment were intrusted by Candaules to this person, and to him he was wont to extol the surpassing beauty of his wife. So matters went on for a while. At length, one day, Candaules, for he was fated to end ill, thus addressed his follower: 'I see thou dost not credit what I tell thee of my lady's loveliness; but come now, since men's ears are less credulous than their eyes, contrive some means whereby thou mayest behold her,'" contrary to our customs. Gyges was amazed at the proposition to do the fair lady wrong, and endeavored to persuade the king from such a disgraceful course. He quoted a proverb against the king's proposal, and professed his unlimited confidence in the king's word. The king thereupon became so urgent that Gyges feared to offend him, and yielded to his plan.

Candaules concealed Gyges in his chamber, but

"as he was passing out she saw him, and instantly divining what had happened, she neither screamed, . . . nor even appeared to have noticed aught, purposing to take vengeance upon the husband who had so affronted her." The next morning, choosing some of the most faithful from among her retinue and disclosing to them the disgrace to which she had been subjected, and announcing her determination to secure summary vengeance, she summoned Gyges into her presence. He obeyed, supposing that she wished to confer with him, and not suspecting that she knew aught of what had occurred. She addressed him in these words: "Take thy choice, Gyges, of two courses which are open to thee. Slay Candaules and thereby become my lord and obtain the Lydian throne, or die this moment in his room." Gyges besought the queen to release him from so hard a choice, but she remained inexorable. Gyges must slay the king in his own bed.

"All was then prepared for the attack, and when night fell Gyges, seeing that he had no retreat or escape, but must absolutely either slay Candaules, or himself be slain, followed his mistress into the sleeping-room. She placed a dagger in his hand and hid him carefully behind the self-same door. Then Gyges, when the king had fallen asleep, entered privily into the chamber and struck him dead. Thus did the wife and kingdom of Candaules pass into the possession of his follower Gyges, of whom Archilochus, the Parian, who lived about the same time, made mention in a poem written in iambic trimeter verse." *

The historian relates how the seven noble embassadors of Megabazus to the court of Amyntas the Macedonian lost their lives for the audacity and wantonness they displayed at the feast " when the meal was over and they were all set to the drinking." †

Xerxes, " merry with wine," sent for Queen Vashti —" the best "—that he might dazzle his guests with her beauty. She must come in brilliant attire and with the " crown royal " upon her head, to submit herself to the impudent gaze of half-drunken nobles. Her " crown " was probably a tall stiff cap set with large jewels like that of Mousa, the Parthian queen, which appears on a coin of her son Phraataces. ‡

Upon ordinary occasions the queen may have been accustomed to take her meals with the king, § but not at public feasts. She was now presiding at the entertainment of the women in the palace. " The summons probably found her with a crowd of female guests before her. She might have been loath at another time to obey; but while they looked on, it was a severer trial to be required to abdicate her dignity and, confessing her royal state *his* bounty, to cast, as it were, her crown before his footstool." ‖

---

* Herodotus, i, 8–12. † *Ibid.*, v, 8.
‡ Rawlinson, *The Sixth Oriental Monarchy*, p. 220.
§ Herodotus, ix, 110. ‖ Tyrwhitt.

None but a Xerxes would have thus broken in upon the order of the entertainment, and humbled the queen in the eyes of all the noble women of the empire. The command was very inopportune. A more serious objection was that to obey the king's command were to do that which, if not positively forbidden by law, was certainly forbidden by custom. The social customs of a thousand years cannot be easily broken. If the king were to command, and that without reason and against all law, and she to obey blindly and mechanically, she were not a help-meet, not a woman, but a convenient ornament to be exhibited at the king's pleasure. Such extravagance and folly were not known in history, and they outraged the established customs of the age! The applause of the revelers would have been her degradation. After this, according to the feelings of the times, she could not have been looked upon as a virtuous matron. Xerxes in his sober moments would have been the first to condemn the folly. Not only would Vashti have been dishonored as a woman, as a mother, and as a queen, and her reputation threatened, but also her royal husband would have shared the disgrace.

Was not the king mad to issue such a command? Yes; wine had stolen away his brain. "It is not for kings, O Lemuel! it is not for kings to drink wine; nor for princes strong drink: lest they drink, and forget the law, and pervert the judgment of any of the afflicted." Prov. xxxi, 4. Wine was in and wit was out. Had there been no wine at the feast the king would have been saved a crying disgrace.

"The drinking was according to the law; none did compel: for so the king had appointed to all the officers of his house, that they should do according to every man's pleasure."

"He respected their national habits, and did not forget that some of the mountaineer Persian tribes, which retained the simplicity and strictness of their ancient customs, were famous for their temperance."* If the king yielded to the wishes of the temperate and issued the irreversible mandate, "No compelling," he also gave full license to the intemperate. "We are not told in the present passage that the king, on this occasion, exceptionally permitted moderation, especially to such of his guests as were, according to their ancestral customs, addicted to moderation, and who would else have been compelled to drink immoderately. For the words with which this verse concludes, while they imply also a permission to each to drink as little as he chose, are specially intended to allow every one to take much." †

While permitting moderation, the meaning was "that the guests in a courageous and vigorous carousing should show their appreciation of the liberal hospitality of the king, and at the same time evince their ability to do something in their drinking worthy of the royal table." ‡

---

* Wordsworth. † Bertheau. ‡ Lange.

Since the guests doubtless vied with the great king, there must have been at this feast many who were mighty to drink wine.

Anciently, as in modern times, wine wrought ruin wherever it went. The monuments of Egypt picture the drunkenness of the people. At Denderah was held a drinking feast, and the goddess of drunkenness was worshiped. Drunkenness threatened the ruin of the Chinese empire more than a thousand years before Christ. About B. C. 1116 the emperor of China felt impelled to publish an edict called "The Announcement about Drunkenness." The Indians in the time of the Vedas were cursed with this curse. The Assyrians drank wine. Babylon fell while her defender and his court were engaged in a drunken carousal. In the time of Christ the Corinthians were usually introduced on the stage in a state of intoxication. Rome was cursed with drunkenness and debauchery. Palestine was swallowed up of strong drink.

Total abstinence then, as now, was the sovereign remedy. The Institutes of Manu enjoined it upon Brahman priests. It was imperative in Buddhism. It gave strength to the arm of the Lacedæmonians. It organized the Rechabites and Nazarites of Palestine. Total abstinence was the practice of the Essenes of Judea and the Theraputæ of Egypt. The Milesian and Cean maidens drank no wine.

The seeds of intemperance are planted in the home. Wine and brandy are used in modern cookery.

They find a permanent and prominent place in the book of household receipts. Children are early accustomed to their flavor. Liquors are always included in the list of family medicines. Patients use alcohol as a remedy long after its necessity, as determined by the judgment of competent medical authority, has ceased. Resort is had to alcohol as the panacea for all ills. Without physicians' prescriptions liquors are freely taken, and recommended to young and old alike. The bill of fare at public houses includes a long wine list. Wine, cider, and other intoxicating beverages are found in the cellar and pantry of private homes. Wine is placed on the board at fashionable suppers, and wine and beer sparkle and foam on the family table. Thus from his earliest years the child is made familiar with the appearance and presence of wine, becomes acquainted with its taste, takes it in his medicine when sick, and in his food when well, learns to think of it as not only harmless, but positively nutritious and healthful and medicinal; considers its use as a sure test of manliness; is urged to drink by all the power of social and parental example, and is invited to its pleasures by all the fascination of fair promise appealing to the lust of the flesh, the lust of the eye, and the pride of life, with a persuasive eloquence most difficult to resist. No wonder that with such a system of education and discipline the thousands fall. Reformation in the home is of prime importance. Wives and mothers share with husbands and fathers the responsibility of the drunkenness that curses the earth.

Not all the wines of antiquity were intoxicating. Some were certainly sweet, and produced no intoxicating effect. The chief butler's dream in Genesis accurately represents one of the ways in which wine was made in Egypt. A picture exhumed at Pompeii represents Bacchus squeezing clusters of grapes and catching the juice in a wine-cup. Dr. Ebers found a picture on the walls of the temple of Edfu representing a king standing with a cup in his hand, and this inscription underneath: "They press grapes into the water and the king drinks." The Greeks and Romans were acquainted with the unfermented juice of the grape. The ancients could prevent or arrest fermentation.

The wines of the Bible are not all intoxicating. But we need not depend on a lexicographical and etymological argument. The Bible is the best text-book on temperance which has ever been published. It furnishes the awful examples of Noah, Lot, the carousers at Belshazzar's feast, and at the more brilliant banquet of Xerxes, in "Shushan the palace." Nabal the churlish died ten days after a drunken feast. Absalom invited Ammon, the king's son, to a sheep-shearing feast, got him drunk, and then slew him. Joel charges the ungodly with having sold "a girl for wine, that they might drink." The wine of the heathen is "the poison of dragons." A woe is pronounced upon the drunkards of Ephraim. Those who are mighty to drink wine and mingle strong drink, and whoever gives his neighbor drink and makes him drunken, can look for but labor and sorrow and woe. Those who rise early in the morning to drink, and continue late at night in drunken revelry, are under the curse of God. The exhortation is given, "Be not among wine-bibbers," and the Christian is commanded not to eat with one who is called a brother, if he be a drunkard. Life-like pictures are given of drunkenness and its fruits. We see the unsteady step, the reeling form, the drunken fall, the feast of wine, the subsequent sickness, and the vomit and filth. We hear the rude joke, the boisterous laugh, and the idiotic shout. We note the disputes, contentions, senseless babblings, roused passions, street fights, aimless wanderings, uncertain vision, wounds, poverty, rags, sorrow, and woe. We learn that wine is a mocker, and that strong drink is raging, and that it is the height of folly to be deceived. We hear it declared that no drunkard shall inherit the kingdom of heaven. The whole spirit of the Bible is opposed to intemperance.

O rum, how dost thou curse the world! Thou dost devour the wealth of the people. Thou dost undermine the foundations of society, invade and control halls of legislation and justice, and set at defiance all laws, human and divine. Thou dost enter the home of peace, purity, and happiness and smite it with thy black wings; forthwith peace is gone,

THE BANQUET OF WINE. 77

purity, weeping and heart-broken, disappears, and happiness is seen no more. Thou dost enter the heart of the husband and he becomes a monster; thou dost enter the heart of the wife and she becomes a demoness. Thou dost steal bread from the mouths of famishing children, snatch clothing from their backs, put out the fire on their hearths, tear down the dwelling from over their heads, paint misery upon their fair features, and turn them out in the fury of the wintry storm to beg in the streets. Thou dost turn joy into sorrow, light into darkness, laughter into mourning, and gladsome songs into the wail of woe, the cry of anguish, the shriek of horror, the sob of grief, the groan of suppressed agony, and loud lamentation—the unavailing remedy of a breaking heart. Thou dost make one an idiot, another a pauper, the third a madman, the fourth a murderer, and the fifth a suicide. For one thou dost prepare the assassin's dagger, for another the burglar's tools, for the third the poisoner's cup, and for the fourth the robber's fatal shot. Like some treacherous Joab, thou dost feign an interest in the health of Amasa, proffer the kiss of friendship, and then smite him with thy sword in the fifth rib. Like some deceitful Delilah, thou dost lull Samson to sleep in thy lap, and then deliver him, shorn of his strength, into the hand of the uncircumcised Philistines. Like some fiery Jael, thou dost allure Sisera by thy blandishments; he enters thy tent; thou dost give him milk to drink; thou dost prepare for him a couch and cover him with a mantle, and then when securely locked in slumber thou with heavy hammer dost send a nail crashing through his temples. Like some fair siren, thou dost charm by thy songs and win by thy smiles, and when thy victim is tempted to thy embrace, thou dost leap with him into the black gulf of perdition. Thou art the foe of modesty, chastity, and virtue. Thou dost rob the eye of its brilliancy, the cheek of its healthful hue, the voice of its clarion clearness, the lips of their color, the breath of its sweetness, the tongue of its articulation, the features of their expression, the brain of its intelligence, the right hand of its cunning, the heart of its affections, the blood of its purity, the nerves of their tone, the muscles of their obedience, the step of its elasticity, the sensibilities of their delicacy, the reason of its power, the judgment of its accuracy, the conscience of its command, the will of its strength, and the man of his humanity. Thou dost fill the asylums, poor-houses, prisons, penitentiaries, and jails. Thou dost plant diseases in the human frame, eat away the lives of men, and dig their graves. Inspired by thee, the husband slays the wife of his bosom, and the father his darling only son. Thou hast slain more than famine, war, and pestilence. Thou hast devoured millions of souls, and yet thy cursed maw is insatiable. Thou dost degrade man, created in the image of God, to the level of a brute. Thou dost bar the road to heaven and doom thy victims to everlasting despair. Thy awful, thy blood-dripping trophies, displayed on every hand, strike all the soul with horror. Thou demon of the pit, with all my being I curse thee!

IV.

FOLLY, ANGER, DIVORCE.

"The queen Vashti refused to come at the king's commandment."—Esther i, 12.

"If it please the king, let there go a royal commandment from him, and let it be written among the laws of the Persians and the Medes, that it be not altered, That Vashti come no more before king Ahasuerus; and let the king give her royal estate unto another that is better than she.—Esther i, 19.

"The court of the Sassanian kings, especially in the later period of the empire, was arranged upon a scale of almost unexampled grandeur and magnificence. The robes worn by the great king were beautifully embroidered, and covered with gems and pearls, which in some representations may be counted by hundreds. The royal crown, which could not be worn, but was hung from the ceiling by a gold chain exactly over the head of the king when he took his seat in his throne-room, is said to have been adorned with a thousand pearls, each as large as an egg. The throne itself was of gold, and was supported on four feet, each formed of a single enormous ruby. The great throne-room was ornamented with enormous columns of silver, between which were hangings of rich silk or brocade. The vaulted roof presented to the eye representations of the heavenly bodies, the sun, the moon, and the stars; while globes, probably of crystal, or of burnished metal, hung suspended from it at various heights, lighting up the dark space as with a thousand lusters." *

Accounts of the more modern Persian courts assist us in our estimation of their ancient splendor. Every thing connected with the reign of Xerxes was grand and imposing. The Persians of his army " were adorned with the greatest magnificence." "They glittered all over with gold, vast quantities of which they wore about their persons. They were followed by litters, wherein rode their concubines, and by a numerous train of attendants handsomely dressed. Camels and sumpter-beasts carried their provision, apart from that of the other soldiers." †

At the close of the battle of Platæa, by order of Pausanius, "the Helots went, and spread themselves through the camp, wherein were found many tents richly adorned with furniture of gold and silver, many couches covered with plates of the same, and many golden bowls, goblets, and other drinking vessels. On the carriages were bags containing silver and golden kettles; and the bodies of the slain furnished bracelets and chains, and scimiters with golden

---

* Rawlinson, *The Seventh Oriental Monarchy*, vol. ii, pp. 301, 302.
† Herodotus, vii, 83.

6

ornaments—not to mention embroidered apparel, of which no one made any account." *

Xerxes was inspired only by the most selfish and unscrupulous ambition. He sought his own glory, and was not careful of the means employed. He sought fame, and fed on flattery and display. He exercised unlimited power, and his riches commanded the worship of his subjects. He lived in extravagant self-complacency. His vanity—swelling, costly, and intolerably burdensome—knew no bounds.

Excited with wine, he commanded that Queen Vashti be brought into the presence of his half-drunken guests that they might behold her beauty and praise her loveliness, "for she was fair to look upon." It was an outrage on all the customs of the empire.

The king awaits the return of the seven chamberlains. They are called in the Septuagint "deacons." Mehuman, the leader—if the *m* be omitted—may have been Haman. They do not return. The guests are in anxious expectancy and are already thinking of proper terms in which to compliment the queenly beauty and flatter her royal husband. And now the chamberlains return, but without Vashti. The king and his guests are amazed. Uncertain of the issue, the chamberlains explain, "the queen Vashti refused to come at the king's commandment." Vashti was

* Herodotus, ix, 80.

doubtless proud of spirit, and instead of returning "a soft answer," and thus perhaps maintaining both her dignity and queenly relation, she met the command of the king with a flat refusal. "Therefore was the king very wroth, and his anger burned in him." Her refusal is to be highly commended, though it might have been given with more diplomacy. Even at Belshazzar's feast the queen was not present until summoned by the hand on the wall. Dan. v, 3, 4.

"Take care that thou be not made a fool by flatterers," says Sir Walter Raleigh, "for even the wisest men are abused by these. Know, therefore, that flatterers are the worst kind of traitors; for they will strengthen thy imperfections, encourage thee in all evils, correct thee in nothing, but so shadow and paint all thy vices and follies as thou shalt never, by their will, discern evil from good, or vice from virtue; and because all men are apt to flatter themselves, to entertain the addition of other men's praises is most perilous. Do not, therefore, praise thyself, except thou wilt be counted a vainglorious fool; neither take delight in the praise of other men, except thou deserve it, and receive it from such as are worthy and honest and will withal warn thee of thy faults; for flatterers have never any virtue; they are ever base, creeping, cowardly persons. A flatterer is said to be a beast that biteth smiling; it is said by Isaiah in this manner: 'My people, they that praise thee, seduce thee, and disorder the paths of thy feet;' and David desired God to cut out the tongue of a flatterer."

Xerxes flattered himself so that the Xerxes created by his vanity was quite another person from the real Xerxes. His desire for praise grew and became insatiable. His courtiers, knowing the only way to royal favor, flattered him in extravagant and most unmeasured terms. They were not sincere, honest, and truthful, for in their hearts they doubtless held him in contempt. But he would listen to nothing save that which fed his vanity. As a slave he was led step by step to the utmost limit of unreasonable and vain self-gratification. He became a fool, and prostituted his crown and his queen to mere low spectacular show. By the queen's refusal, his pride, gratified, encouraged, fed, praised, and pampered, was touched at a most vital point.

The great king was surrounded by wealth, splendor, and glory. There were gathered to him all that was beautiful to the eye, all that was grateful to the taste, and all that could rejoice the heart. He ruled many powerful, rich, and renowned nations. He dwelt in a great city, his palaces were of surpassing beauty, and he commanded every luxury. Obsequious servants were attentive to do his bidding, the feast was in progress, and all lips were full of his praise. Fair ladies and Persian beauties, gem-adorned and diamond-crowned, were entertained right royally by his matchless queen. But happiness is not found in golden halls. True pleasure flows from a pure heart. The praise of his guests, though without stint, does not satisfy the king. He determines to call forth still higher terms of praise, and all his joy is turned to anger and chagrin.

The great king is an absolute monarch. He controls the vast wealth of one hundred and twenty-seven provinces, possesses the power of life and death over the inhabitants, can call to arms millions of men, and acknowledges no rival. His personal will is the supreme and unquestioned law, vast rivers are insufficient to quench the thirst of his armies, no enemy can escape his power, and he is like a god upon the earth. No more absolute, independent, and commanding a worldly position were possible. This king of absolute power is defeated and humiliated in his own capital, in his own palace, in his own family, and by his own wife. The love and loyalty of one woman alone will bring more true happiness, more sunny contentment, and more wealth of soul than the scepter of a Xerxes.

"The queen Vashti refused to come at the king's commandment." The king did not dream of such a rebuff, and he has no power to conquer her insubordinate spirit. What shall he do? The eyes of the Persian empire are upon him. He has slain lesser offenders. The seven chamberlains and all the convivial company must have expected an explosion of his wrath and an edict for her immediate execution. Artabanus, at this same feast, advised against the Grecian expedition, and Xerxes, full of wrath, replied: "Artabanus, thou art my father's brother—that shall save thee from receiving the due meed of thy silly words. One shame, however, I will lay upon thee, coward and faint-hearted as thou art—thou shalt not come with me to fight these Greeks, but shalt tarry here with the women." When a great storm broke the bridge of the Hellespont he "commanded that the overseers of the work should lose their heads." To avenge himself upon Pythius, who had dared to ask for one of his five sons to be dismissed from the army to be the stay of his declining years, Xerxes seized the eldest son, cut his body in twain, and caused the army to march out between the two halves. He most barbarously ill-treated the body of his dead enemy, the brave Leonidas.* When Darius was about to set out on an expedition against Scythia, a Persian named Œobazus, whose three sons were in the army, prayed the king to permit one to remain at home. The king replied "that he would allow them all to remain," and bade his attendants put the three sons to death. † It is a dangerous thing to arouse the wrath of a Persian king. His anger may be unjust, selfish, and cruel, no one can reason with him or stay his fury. A brave and spirited

---

* Herodotus, vii, 11, 35, 38, 238. † *Ibid.*, iv, 84.

woman was Vashti, to dare the wrath of Xerxes, even to preserve her womanly modesty and dignity.

A greater man than Xerxes might, under the circumstances, have forgiven the queen. Xerxes could not forgive. He might have postponed the consideration of the question till some future time, but his blood was up, and he determined upon speedy action. Yet he seemed to have been partially sobered by this unexpected turn in the pleasures of the banquet, and would act only under the semblance at least of law. He sought counsel, for in the multitude of counselors there is wisdom. A good counselor should be a man of wisdom, experience, and reputation, that confidence may be placed in his judgment. He must advise without fear or flattery. He must be unselfish, just, and reasonable, as seeking the best good of his friend. Such a counselor may be of inestimable value to a ruler who is wise to listen to advice.

Now below the king, in his court, were six privileged families, higher in rank than the other nobles. These with the royal family—the Achæmenidæ—would make seven great families. They were fellow-conspirators when Darius Hystaspis was raised to the throne.* Only from these seven families could the king select his wives. The Behistun Inscription confirms Herodotus with respect to those families. They were "the seven princes of Persia and Media, which

* Herodotus, iii, 84.

saw the king's face," and "the king and his seven counselors." Esther i, 14; Ezra vii, 14. At their pleasure they were privileged to advise and to recommend important measures, for the execution of which they became in some degree responsible. When the king was not in the female apartments they could enter his presence without being introduced by an usher.* In all ceremonies they had precedence by virtue of rank. Officers of the court were distinguished by a wand about three feet long, or by an ornament resembling a lotus blossom, which was also seen sometimes in the hand of the king. They also wore golden collars and golden earrings, and sometimes carried a dagger in their girdle.

These seven distinguished counselors—Carshena, Shethar, Admatha, Tarshish, Meres, Marsena, and Memucan—who "sat the first in the kingdom," descended from the families of the seven conspirators who placed Darius upon the throne, or, at least, stood in a similar relation to the king. They bore names of "a general Persian cast." Marsena may be the famous general, Mardonius, and Admatha may be Artabanus, the uncle of Xerxes. These men were called upon to advise the king in his unexpected difficulty.

But they were to be associated in their deliberation with others—"the wise men who knew the times." The latter were the astrologers and magi. Astyages,

---

* Herodotus, iii, 118.

the son of Cyaxares, consulted the magi concerning a dream which had thrown him into great terror. According to these wise men the dream prophesied the birth and empire of Cyrus. Another dream was read in a similar manner. When Cyrus had escaped the plot formed for his destruction, and rejoiced in his young life, Astyages again consulted the magi concerning the probable fulfillment of the dream.*

Xerxes had had a dream while celebrating this same feast. "He dreamed that he was crowned with a branch of an olive tree, and that boughs spread out from the olive branch and covered the whole earth; then suddenly the garland, as it lay upon his brow, vanished." He consulted the magi and was told "that its meaning reached to the whole earth, and that all mankind would become his servants." † When his army began its march from Sardis toward Abydos "the sun suddenly quitted his seat in the heavens and disappeared, though there were no clouds in sight, but the sky was clear and serene." The magi were called upon to interpret the portent.

During the storm off Artemisium the magi offered victims to the winds, and charmed them by the help of conjurors. ‡ Oriental sovereigns frequently sought the interpretation of dreams and prodigies from their priests. Gen. xli, 8; Dan. ii, 2; iv, 6. The wise men of Babylon gave counsel according to celestial

* Herodotus, i, 107, 120.   † *Ibid.*, vii, 19.   ‡ *Ibid.*, vii, 191.

phenomena. Dan. ii, 27; v, 15; Isa. xliv, 25; xlvii, 13; Jer. l, 35.'

Xerxes was fond of asking advice, but would brook nothing which did not coincide with his own inclination.* Though his own will was the supreme law of the empire, yet now he turns to the wise men and counselors, "for so was the king's manner toward all that knew law and judgment," and asks, "What shall we do unto the queen Vashti, according to law, because she hath not performed the commandment of the king Ahasuerus by the chamberlains?" The wise men and counselors retire for consultation. It is a time of anxiety to both king and guests. The queen is in suspense, yet determined and resolute. The noble ladies whom she entertains are in tears. The wine has ceased to flow. A bright morning is often followed by a dark evening.

The king's advisers have a delicate task to perform. They are placed in a dilemma. Whichever way they turn they are in a perilous position. If they justify, or excuse, or lessen the gravity of the offense of the queen, it will be at the risk of their lives. If they condemn the queen, as they feel compelled to do, what punishment shall they recommend? The king passionately loves the beautiful Vashti. They dare not recommend the penalty of death, yet if she live and ever again be brought into a position of authority,

* Herodotus, vii, 8, 11, 48, 234; viii, 101.

her judges will in all probability lose their heads. Her character—if she be the same as the Amestris of Herodotus—is equal to any severity of vengeance.

It were not a light thing to fall into the hands of a Persian queen. When Parysatis, the mother of Cyrus the younger and Artaxerxes II., had secured possession of the Carian who claimed to have slain Cyrus, "She delivered him to the executioner, with orders to torture him for ten days, and then to tear out his eyes, and pour molten brass into his ears, till he expired." Mithridates, when under the influence of wine, confessed to have slain Cyrus, and she condemned him to the punishment of *the boat*, which is too horrible to relate. At a game of dice with the king she won a eunuch, and chose Mesabates, who, according to Persian custom, had cut off the head and right hand of Cyrus, and caused this Mesabates to be flayed, his body to be fixed on three stakes, and his skin to be stretched out by itself.

No counselors were ever called upon to give advice under more perplexing circumstances. The only solution of the difficult problem presented to them is to spare the life of the queen and yet to place her beyond all means of ever doing her judges personal harm. The laws of the Persians and Medes change not. Many allusions in Greek authors confirm this point. They can place her under the ban of this unchangeable law. Having reached this decision they appoint Memucan their spokesman and return to the presence of the king. He frames his answer with the skill of a crafty diplomat:

"Vashti the queen hath not done wrong to the king only, but also to all the princes, and to all the people that are in all the provinces of the king Ahasuerus. For this deed of the queen shall come abroad unto all woman, so that they shall despise their husbands in their eyes, when it shall be reported, The king Ahasuerus commanded Vashti the queen to be brought in before him, but she came not. Likewise shall the ladies of Persia and Media say this day unto all the king's princes, which have heard of the deed of the queen. Thus shall there arise too much contempt and wrath."

In this artful exaggeration of the queen's fault powerful testimony is borne to the unmeasured reach of influence. This is a most important truth. No deed which is done ever dies and is forgotten. The words which we speak live on and on after our bodies have turned to ashes. The dusty grave cannot cover a life. Influence is subtle and deep, and travels far and wide. This influence, silent, magnetic, growing, pervading, is a wonderful thing. No one can live without exerting an influence which shall work for others either weal or woe, and this influence shall belt the earth. Thoughts, words, acts are immortal. They are all written somewhere, and we shall meet them again. Mighty are the marvels they shall do as they roll onward through the eternities, widening and deepening in their range and power, blighting or blessing in their course.

The higher the position, the wider the influence. All eyes look to the queen. There should be purity at the head of a government. The wives and husbands of the Persian empire are to be involved in this act of disobedience.

Weighing the offense, the tribunal advises: "If it please the king, let there go a royal commandment from him, and let it be written among the laws of the Persians and the Medes, that it be not altered, That Vashti come no more before king Ahasuerus; and let the king give her royal estate unto another that is better than she. And when the king's decree, which he shall make, shall be published throughout all his empire (for it is great), all the wives shall give to their husbands honor, both to great and small."

Thus the queen's act is made the blackest crime, and the semblance of guarding morality and justice is made to hide hypocrisy, injustice, and violence.

"Here and in the account of the honors paid to Mordecai the English word 'honor' is not at all adequate to the translating of the Hebrew." The original word "retains its meaning of costliness or preciousness, designating that which is valuable because it is scarce—that which is difficult to get and easy to lose. The idea here is that the women will come to regard their husbands as peculiarly valuable and precarious possessions, against the alienation of which they need to guard with peculiar care." *

"And the saying pleased the king and the princes; and the king did according to the word of Memucan: for he sent letters into all the king's provinces, into every province according to the writing thereof, and to every people after their language, that every man should bear rule in his own house, and that it should be published according to the language of every people."

Much more was doubtless contained in these "letters," translated into the various languages of the different satrapies—a custom preserved to us in the bilingual and trilingual inscriptions discovered in eastern lands—but sacred story contains but two important mandates: that the man bear rule in his own house, and that only the language of the husband be used in the family.

"This decree," says Rawlinson, "has been called 'absurd' and 'quite unnecessary in Persia.' † If the criticism were allowed, it would be sufficient to observe that many absurd things were done by Xerxes.‡ But it may be questioned whether the decree was unnecessary. The undue influence of women in domestic and even in public affairs is a feature of the

* Willis J. Beecher.   † Davidson.   ‡ Herod., viii, 35; ix, 108–111.

ancient Persian monarchy. Herodotus tells us that Atossa 'completely ruled' Darius.* Xerxes himself was, in his later years, shamefully subject to Amestris.† The example of the court would naturally affect the people. The decree, therefore, would seem to have been not so much an idle and superfluous act as an ineffectual protest against a real and growing evil."

Nehemiah met with a difficulty which the second order was aimed to remove. "In those days also saw I Jews that had married wives of Ashdod, of Ammon, and of Moab: and their children spake half in the speech of Ashdod, and could not speak in the Jews' language, but according to the language of each people." Neh. xiii, 23, 24. The children naturally learning the tongue of the mother, she could wield over them an influence of which the father would be totally ignorant. In Persia man made woman a slave instead of a companion and a helpmeet, and was enslaved with a worse slavery in turn.

Vashti is divorced, the wise men and counselors and princes are satisfied, the wrath of the king is appeased, messengers are on their way to carry the edicts of Xerxes to the utmost provinces of the kingdom, the great feast is ended, noble guests return to their homes, affairs of state proceed as usual, and the excitement caused by the disobedient queen has passed away.

* Herodotus, vii, 3. † *Ibid.*, ix, 111.

V.

LOVE AND HOME.

"Let there be fair young virgins sought for the king."—Esther ii, 2.

"A Church within a Church, a republic within a republic, a world within a world, is spelled by four letters—H-o-m-e! If things go right there, they go right every-where; if things go wrong there, they go wrong every-where. The door-sill of the dwelling-house is the foundation of Church and State. A man never gets higher than his own garret or lower than his own cellar. In other words, domestic life overarches and undergirds all other life. The highest house of congress is the domestic circle; the rocking-chair in the nursery is higher than a throne." *

"Domestic society is the seminary of social affections, the cradle of sensibility, where the first elements are acquired of that tenderness and humanity which cement society together; and were they entirely extinguished the whole fabric of social institutions would be dissolved. Families are so many centers of attraction, which preserve mankind from being scattered and dissipated by the repulsive powers of selfishness." †

* Talmage. † Robert Hall.

The true wife and mother is the center around which the family affections twine. Love is the attractive power which binds all together in these most holy of all human relations. All forms of socialism, liberalism, and other errors of like character threaten the destruction of the whole social fabric. The position of woman, the sacredness of the marriage relation, and the purity of the home life, measure in all lands, not only the breadth and depth of healthful intellectual culture and the condition of civilization and religious development, but also the stability of government and the sovereignty of law.

There are two important departures from the model of a true family and home.

The plurality of husbands is a most ancient institution. An excerpt taken from an old Chinese record, belonging to the archaic period of Chinese history, shows that this custom was then prevalent in the celestial empire:

"The husbands of the woman took counsel, and said: 'Which of us shall fight the tiger?' Wong-Lee said, 'I am the largest and strongest; I can best fight him. I will go.' Wong-He-Lim said, 'I am the weakest; therefore I should go. For if Wong-Lee is killed by the tiger, our loss is very great. But if I am killed no harm is done.' So Wong-Lee and Wong-He-Lim went out together and encountered the tiger, and after a terrible fight killed him. And when they came back, the woman and the other husbands were glad, and sacrificed chickens and pigs."

This system of polyandry—which may have grown out of some more primitive condition—has prevailed widely in the early history of the race. In the present age the plurality of wives is more common. Polygamy is still a cancer upon the social organism.

Roman law gave the wife equal rank with her husband, but placed the children under his control. The relation of concubinage was also recognized in law, and it was not till the Council of Trent that the Church dealt with the subject in the spirit of thorough reform.

The Old Testament recognizes a conjugal relation inferior to the marriage relation. While it may be said that the position of the wife was less honorable in early Oriental life than in modern western life, it is also true that the position of the concubine was less degraded.

In early times the Persian kings seem to have had but three or four wives, and but one of those was designated by the title of "queen" and was *the wife* in the highest meaning of the term. The queen wore a royal crown and was the acknowledged head of the female department of the palace. The other women of the palace recognized her queenly dignity by prostrating themselves in her presence. Her apparel was most gorgeous, her ornaments many and costly, her revenues enormous, and her power over the king very great. The other wives were raised little above the concubines. The king could legally marry in but seven of the noble families of Persia, though the royal WILL was above all law. Each subordinate wife, doubtless, had her own attendants and her own suite of apartments. The royal harem grew in importance in the later history of the Persians.

The virgins occupied the first house of the women during the twelve months of purification, or until called into the presence of the king. After this they went to the second house of the women. All were placed under the charge of faithful eunuchs, who kept them guarded in strictest seclusion. The king's harem was filled with the most beautiful women of the kingdom, who, sometimes several hundred in number, accompanied their lord both in his wars and in his hunting expeditions. Quintus Curtius tells us that Darius was accompanied in his warlike expeditions by three hundred and sixty-five concubines, all with the equipage of queens.

In Shushan the palace the second house of the women was separated from the king's house by a court. There were separate suites of apartments for the virgins, the concubines, and the queen and other wives. While chamberlains had charge of the first and second, the queen herself was paramount in the third.

The queen-mother was superior in authority even to the queen. She kept her own ensigns of power, and was often proud and domineering. Whenever the king and queen dined together, the queen-mother sat at the royal table and occupied a position above the monarch, while the queen herself was seated below in a more humble position. She had her own commodious suite of apartments and ample revenues at her disposal. She procured the royal pardon for criminals, or sheltered them in her own apartments, while she secretly poisoned or openly executed those of whom she was jealous, or against whom she was angry. The king himself often fell completely under her control, when she would prove herself most dangerous to the peace of the court and of the empire.

Persian inscriptions and sculptures are silent in regard to women. The female form could not be lawfully represented, and women must not be named nor yet seen in public. It was a capital crime to address a royal concubine, or even to pass the litter in which one was borne. Married women were not permitted to see even their nearest male relatives. In Persia to-day a man is insulted if asked about the health of his wife. Vashti's refusal to obey the command of the king exhibited not only her womanly delicacy, and wifely modesty, and queenly dignity, but also her loyalty to custom.

The word *eunuch* means etymologically "bed-keeper"—one who has charge of sleeping apartments. The unnatural and barbarous custom of employing eunuchs could have had its home nowhere save in the despotic East. Beautiful captives, both those of tender years and those who had attained maturity, were purchased or captured or seized for this office and degradation.

This class of servants is often represented on the Assyrian monuments—warriors, scribes, priests, full-faced, beardless, double-chinned. These unhappy wretches, having no social interests, no family hopes, and no prospects better than slavery, were the props of absolute government, the tools of despotism, the guardians of the monarch's person, the keepers of the harem, and the sole witnesses of all the private and unguarded acts of their royal master. They frequently rose to positions of great influence, were appointed ambassadors to foreign courts, and became the custodians of most important trusts. Treated frequently with aversion and ridicule, they became stern and unfeeling in the exercise of authority, and introduced tyranny and licentiousness. Courage, gentleness, and shame too often gave way to melancholy, malice, and cruelty. Not a few, unable to endure their cruel fate, sought release in self-destruction.

This unfortunate class, the natural outgrowth of polygamy, was large and powerful in the Persian empire. The king chose them as chief advisers, officers of his court, generals of his armies, and educators of his children. Through their influence were born many dark plots, traitorous conspiracies, and bloody assassinations, which disgrace the pages of history. Barbarous villainies were connected with the nefarious traffic in eunuchs. The story of Panionius of Chios, and the awful revenge of Hermotimus, are too horrible to repeat.*

Such was the family of a Persian king—the king himself, the queen mother, the queen, the other wives, the concubines, the virgins and the chamberlains—while a multitude of servants, guests, visitors, ambassadors, hostages, travelers, princes, and high officers thronged the royal palace. This was not a family, and the great palace was not a home. Love could not bear sway, nor happiness abide, in "Shushan the palace."

A family is one man and one woman united in perpetual wedlock, each giving to the other permanent, unchanging, undivided, exclusive, and full affection and devotion, and the children of this relationship; who are the objects of tenderest parental love and care, which they repay with all the warmth of filial affection while they extend to each other full and hearty fraternal love. Conjugal affection is the basis of the family, and there is no family where this

* Herodotus, viii, 105, 106.

is absent. Persons united by worldly self-interest do not constitute a family. Neither property, nor position in society, nor fancy, nor fascination, can take the place of genuine love. Just so far as a man and woman are influenced to marry from any other motive than pure affection, just to that extent the union is contrary to the law of nature, the law of reason, the law of conscience, and the law of God. There should be honesty, and not deception, in the social intercourse preceding marriage.

The ideal family and the ideal home are pictured only in the Bible and realized only in Christian lands. Such a home is an object-lesson of religious doctrine and practice. Here the truths of Christianity find expression in Christian lives. There is a church in every genuine Christian home. The husband and father is the family priest. The home is the foundation of society and of civil government. Christian children are educated for loyal and enlightened citizenship.

The home furnishes us with the very choicest illustrations and symbols of heaven. Heaven is the home of the Christian. We pray to "Our Father which art in heaven." We are his children and his heirs. In our Father's house are many mansions.

The existence of such a family as was that of Xerxes is sufficient of itself to explain all his calamities.

The great banquet is ended. The guests from distant provinces have returned to their homes. The beautiful Vashti has retired in disgrace under the royal displeasure. The king is left alone with his court. The excitement of the banquet of wine has worn away. Xerxes reflects upon the feasting and drinking and revelry of one hundred and four score and seven days, and it brings him no pleasure. His palace has been robbed of its fairest jewel and chiefest charm. He recognizes his divorcement of Vashti as inconsiderate, rash, and unwarranted. He has done the fair queen an irreparable injury, and has brought grievous suffering to his own soul. His anger is appeased and his old love for his queen has returned. He bitterly laments the wrong to which his despotic ambition and selfish vanity have led him, but he cannot retrace his steps. There is no remedy, for "the laws of the Persians and the Medes" change not, however disastrous may be the consequences. He has done evil and he cannot undo it, and it must stand. He would gladly efface from his memory the record of the past revelry, but it is impossible. What he has said and what he has enacted as law are irreversible and indelible.

"He remembered Vashti, and what she had done, and what was decreed against her." She was innocent; he was guilty. His repentance was as speedy as his act was rash. Now his heart goes out after her whom he had so deeply and cruelly wronged! Without her presence the light of his palace is darkness. He is seriously considering her recall. What are "the laws of the Persians and the Medes" to him? His WILL is a higher law. Vashti must return.

The wise men and chief councilors read the king's thoughts. They are alarmed. If Vashti be recalled, their own lives will be forfeited to her rage. If she be not recalled, an explosion of the king's wrath may doom them to death. They must at all hazards prevent the recall of the queen, and at the same time steal away from her the heart of the king. Here is their only safety. Having determined upon their course, they come to the king with the following fair recommendations. "Let there be fair young virgins sought for the king"—those who are beautiful, chaste, young, and marriageable—"and let the king appoint officers in all the provinces of the kingdom, that they may gather together all the fair young virgins unto Shushan the palace, to the house of the women, unto the custody of Hege the king's chamberlain, keeper of the women," or of the virgins who have not yet been presented to the king; "and let their things for purification be given *them;* and let the maiden which pleaseth the king be queen instead of Vashti." —ESTHER ii, 2–4.

Here is safety for themselves and solace for their royal master. The whole empire must feed the king's harem. No one when bidden dare refuse to yield to the king's officers. No parent, though he knows that he will never again see his daughter, dare utter a word of expostulation.

"And the thing pleased the king; and he did so."

And now preparations are made in all the provinces for the vigorous prosecution of the Grecian war. The governors and generals of military renown have received their orders, and, to merit a kingly reward, are anxious to lead their troops to the general rendezvous at Sardis, in "the most gallant array."* Greece is invaded, overwhelming disaster meets the mighty army, the king returns inglorious, and is again in Shushan the palace.

* Herodotus, vii, 26.

VI.

THE QUEENLINESS OF BEAUTY.

"There was a certain Jew whose name *was* Mordecai."—ESTH. ii, 5.
" He brought up Hadassah, that is, Esther, his uncle's daughter."
—ESTHER ii, 7.
" The maid *was* fair and beautiful."—ESTHER ii, 7.

THE captivity of Jehoiachin, the last direct heir of the house of David, one whom God had forsaken, was an occasion of great mourning. The captives are hurried away to a distant land that they know not. Dean Stanley, drawing from the Scriptures, is graphic in his description: " From the top of Lebanon, from the heights of Bashan, from the ridges of Abarim, the widowed country shrieked aloud as she saw the train of her captive king and nobles disappearing in the distant East. From the heights of Hermon, from the top of Mizar, it is no improbable conjecture that the departing king poured that exquisitely plaintive song, in which, from the deep disquietude of his heart, he longs after the presence of God in the temple, and pleads his cause against the impious nation, the treacherous and unjust man, who, in spite of plighted faith, had torn him away from his beloved home. With streaming eyes the Jewish people and prophets still hung on the hope that their lost prince would be speedily restored to them. The gate through which he had left the city was walled up, like that by which the last Moorish king left Granada, and was long known as the gate of Jeconiah. From his captivity, as from a decisive era, the subsequent years of history were reckoned."

Exile must have been a severe punishment to the Jew, bound as he was to his native land not only by the most enthusiastic patriotism, but also by the strongest religious associations and instincts. Palestine was most sacred soil, Jerusalem was the center and home of his religion, and the temple was the most holy place. In a strange land the captive remembered Zion, prayed toward Jerusalem, and lovingly and longingly thought of his own dear country.

JEWISH CAPTIVES.

The exiles whom Nebuchadnezzar led captive to Babylon with Jehoiachin dwelt as a colony on the banks of the Chebar—according to Rawlinson, one of the branches of the Euphrates, near Babylon, but according to Layard the Khabour—and there maintained an organization, consisting of elders and chiefs, with power of acting for the whole body. Most influential among them was Ezekiel, the prophet, the poet, the statesman. Drawing from his surroundings his bold and original figures, luxuriant in eagle-winged lions and human-headed bulls, wheels within wheels, glorious rainbow lights and gigantic forms, now again revealed to our fleshly eyes from the ruins of Nineveh and other Oriental cities, the prophet moves among his fellow-captives and talks to them about the great events in the midst of which they live and act.

But across the great Euphrates, across the desert, he looks, and his spirit yearns for his native land. He sees in prophetic vision the war, the carnage, the devastation, the desolation, and a grief deep and terrible weighs down his loyal soul. The burden of the woes of his country presses heavily upon his heart. Of these things he speaks and writes while he watches anxiously the progress of events. Jerusalem is besieged and falls, and his heart almost breaks.

The prophet, however, was not discouraged. He looked forward to another and better dispensation, when God's spirit should breathe into dry bones and they should live, and stand up, an exceeding great army. He was sure that a greater glory would come to his nation, and there was no cause for despair but rather for good courage. Ezekiel had deep spiritual vision. He saw the Gospel truths. If any man turn away from his wickedness "he shall save his soul alive." Each man must live for himself and each man must die for himself. He believes in the gospel of personal responsibility. Wicked nations, one after the other, fall. He sees their doom. They are destroyed because of their sins. But God will not cast off his own people. His eyes are upon them, and they will repent and be saved.

In Babylon the exiles were educated amid scenes of mighty grandeur and magnificence. The wall of the city is one of the great wonders of the world. The hanging gardens—artificial mountains—are no less wonderful. The great palace of the king is a city within itself. The Temple of Bel, six hundred feet in height, with its seven stages of different colors—black, orange, crimson, gold, deep yellow, brilliant blue, and silver—may well remind them of the Tower of Babel, whose top was to reach to heaven. The magnificent gardens, the gigantic trees, the luxuriant vegetation, the great river, the system of canals, the broad plain carpeted with flowers, the vast commerce, the soldiery with burnished helmet and spear, the officers, "the satraps, captains, pachas, the chief judges, treasurers, judges, counselors, and all the rulers of the provinces," with their splendid costumes and armor—the magicians, sorcerers, astrologers, Chaldeans, the science, the sculpture, the painting, the music, "flute, harp, sackbut, psaltery, dulcimer, and all kinds of music," the activity of trade, "the merchandise of gold, and silver, and precious stones, and of pearls, and fine linen, and purple, and silk, and scarlet, and all thyine wood, and all manner vessels of ivory, and all manner vessels of most precious wood, and of brass, and iron, and marble, and cinnamon, and odors, and ointments, and frankincense, and wine, and oil, and fine flour, and wheat, and beasts, and sheep, and horses, and chariots, and slaves, and souls of men"—these things furnish the school in which the exiles are receiving most valuable tuition. And here dwells Nebuchadnezzar, " whose brightness is excellent," a tree " whose leaves are fair and the fruit thereof much, and in it meat for all," under which the beasts of the field dwell, and upon whose branches the fowls of the air have their habitation—a mighty monarch who can say truthfully · " Is not this great Babylon, that I have built for the house of my kingdom, by the might of my power, and for the honor of my majesty?"

These first exiles are joined by others under Zedekiah, and the two groups doubtless soon blend together. They receive a letter of consolation and instruction from Jeremiah. Prophecies are committed to writing and read to the people. The pen becomes a powerful instrument. The word is read and studied, and its spiritual meaning is revealed. Musicians cheer the sad exiles with songs of Zion, but will not play to satisfy the idle curiosity of their masters. A Psalm commemorates their condition: "By the rivers of Babylon, there we sat down, yea, we wept, when we remembered Zion. We hanged our harps upon the willows in the midst thereof. For there they that carried us away captive required of us a song; and they that wasted us required of us mirth, saying, Sing us one of the songs of Zion. How shall we sing the Lord's song in a strange land? If I forget thee, O Jerusalem, let my right hand forget her cunning. If I do not remember thee, let my tongue cleave to the roof of my mouth; if I prefer not Jerusalem above my chief joy." Psa. cxxxvii, 1–6.

JUDEA CAPTA.

The writings which refer to the period of the captivity show quite fully its dark side. The Israelites are thrown into dungeons with scanty food, they are shamefully insulted and scourged, they are compelled to eat that which to Jewish law is most unclean, they sing mournful songs, and look forward to the time when all their wrongs shall be made right, they cry for deliverance, with eager longing they watch for the morning of that day of triumph which they believe will come, they pour out their prayers from breaking hearts, their tears fall, and they speak of the wickedness of their captors and look to God to avenge himself upon his enemies. And yet they think hopefully of Zion! They pray: "Build thou the walls of Jerusalem. O, that salvation would come out of Zion! When God bringeth back the captivity of his people, Jacob shall rejoice, and Israel shall be glad. God will save Zion, and will build the cities of Judah: that they may dwell there, and have it in possession. Redeem Israel, O God, out of all his troubles."

But there was also a bright side to the captivity. There was a wheel within a wheel—God's providence directed to an end.

When the Babylonian empire fell, the slavery of the captives—it must have been a modified slavery to which some of them had been reduced—this slavery ceased. They were colonists from the beginning. Babylon became the center of Jewish learning and the second capital of their race. Following the advice of their prophets, they acquired homes, property and slaves, and even surrounded themselves with luxuries. Jehoiachin, after a long imprisonment, was released, and maintained with highest honors at public expense. There was even a semblance of independent government, and the exiles had doubtless synagogues in which to worship. Some were appointed to high offices in the government.

The captivity seems to have taught the exiles the importance of spiritual worship. They sought God in prayer, and gave themselves to the study of the Holy Scriptures. They must also have recognized the fact that their God was also the God of all the nations of the world. Their hearts went out in love toward humanity, and they hoped for the redemption of the whole human race.

Cyrus, king of the Medes and Persians, takes Babylon, and the great city, "the praise of the whole earth, the glory of kingdoms, the beauty of the Chaldees' excellency, the lady of kingdoms," is destroyed, never to be inhabited "from generation to generation," a prophecy requiring for its complete fulfillment several hundred years, but whose beginnings were fulfilled before the eyes of the Jewish exiles. And the captive looked for an everlasting kingdom which the Lord of heaven should set up, and which should never be destroyed.

Cyrus is moved by Jehovah to issue a decree permitting the exiles to return to Jerusalem, and many availed themselves of the privilege, though perhaps not more than one sixth of the whole number. Family and business interests influenced the majority to remain. Forty-two thousand besides slaves, under the leadership of twelve chiefs, turn their faces toward Zion, returning with songs and everlasting joy upon their heads. Other groups of pious Jews in later years returned to the land of their fathers' sepulchers. Among these most prominent were Ezra the scribe, the father of preaching; and Nehemiah, the warrior and statesman; both noble reformers.

Of the ten tribes who were carried away into captivity, some returned with the Jews, some embraced the religion of the Assyrians, some amalgamated with the exiles of Judah, and some were scattered abroad and carried the knowledge of the true God to the doors of many heathen nations. The twelve tribes were again united in their exile.

Before the captivity many Israelites had settled in Egypt, and Jews afterward fled from Nebuzaradan to Egypt. Still others established themselves in Sheba in Arabia, where their influence became very great. They were literally "dispersed among the people in all the provinces" of the Persian empire. Whether coming from the kingdom of Israel or from the kingdom of Judah, whether going into enforced or voluntary exile, their influence must have been great in preparing the way of the Lord among the heathen.

Among the noble captives who accompanied Jehoiachin to Babylon was Kish, a Benjamite, from whom the fourth in descent was Mordecai, "who brought up Hadassah, that is, Esther, his uncle's daughter: for she had neither father nor mother, and the maid was fair and beautiful; whom Mordecai, when her father and mother were dead, took for his own daughter." Rawlinson identifies Mordecai, " the son of Jair, the son of Shimei, the son of Kish," with Matacas, whom Ctesias names as the most powerful of the eunuchs in the court of the king during the latter part of his reign. It has been thought that Jair, Shimei, and Kish were not the immediate ancestors of Mordecai, but renowned names in the ancestral line. Jair may have been his father, Shimei the son of Gera who cursed David, and Kish the father of Saul.* This would make Mordecai and his cousin Esther of royal descent. This supposition, however, cannot be pressed. Both were born in exile. Abihail, the father of Esther, was dead. Her mother was also dead, and she was left an orphan in the land of captivity. Fortunate for the beautiful Jewish maiden, she found a protector and father in her cousin Mordecai, who took her " for his own daughter."

"Mordecai was one of those characters which bespeak the hand of a special providence in their formation. Brought up in obscurity, he possessed talents which fitted him for swaying the scepter of empire—wisdom, public spirit, decision, courage, disinterest-

* Keil.

edness, self-command. He was also pious, patriotic, and benevolent." * Mordecai saved the beautiful maiden from many temptations and dangers. He showed himself in every respect a man of God.

"And the maid was fair and beautiful"—graceful in form and bearing, and beautiful in countenance.

"She was called Hadassah—meaning 'myrtle'—because of her sweet disposition and kindly acts, which were compared to the fragrant perfume and ever fresh beauty of the myrtle." It was, doubtless, after she had been introduced to the royal harem that she received, according to the custom of the times, a second, and foreign, name, Esther, which ever afterward became her favorite name. Her matchless beauty suggested this second name, meaning "star." The names Estelle or Stella, and the name of the goddess of love, Istar or Ashtoreth, are from the same root.

The whole universe is bathed in beauty. It gleams in the sea-shell, it glows in the warm sunshine, it plays in the chasing shadows, it toys with the petals of lily and violet, it paints the plumage of bird and the armature of insect, it dances in the hail-shower, it sleeps in the glacier, it is cradled in the silver lake, it sports in the meandering stream, it hides itself in the depths of the ocean and the mountain cave, it ushers in the day as the rosy-fingered daughter of the morning, it rejoices in the flowers of

* McCrie.

spring and the out-pouring wealth of summer, and in the golden grain and luscious fruits of autumn, it arches the sky with the many-colored iris and lights up the northern night with the brilliant electric display of the aurora, it kisses the rose into blushes and drinks nectar from the fairy cup of the lily of the valley, it touches the autumn foliage with its magic brush, and the whole forest becomes one blaze of glory. The light, fleecy clouds, sailing through the air, the crystal and the pearl, the snow-flake, so delicate that it is dissolved by the touch of a fairy's finger, the meadow-grass rolling wave on wave, the tall tree of the forest raising its arms to heaven as if to supplicate blessings, the tearful willow, the stately palm, the confiding vine, the tiny blade of grass, the woody dell—these are most beautiful objects.

The microscope reveals the beauties of the infinitely small; the telescope and the spectroscope bring the distant near. Every smallest atom of matter is running, leaping, and dancing with delight; the worlds above us sing as they fly; galaxies and nebular stardust proclaim the glory of God. Sun and silver moon adorn the sky. The stars walk out as sentinels on the blue pavement; their faces are reflected in the mirror of the waters. The curling smoke climbs upward to heaven, the sun chases the mists from the valleys, the world puts on her green robe, the blanket of night is spread and nature sleeps. The bird sings her beautiful song, the breeze whispers soft and low, the leaf rustles a welcome to the forest solitude, the insect flits in the sunlight and is happy, the lambkin skips and plays, the cattle of a thousand hills rejoice. The fish sports in the sea, the bird in the air, the insect in the dust. Sweet the song of nature's choristers, glad the shout of the waterfall, grand the unwritten music that fills creation. The swallow skims meadow and stream, the eagle with outspread wings soars in the upper air, the tireless humming-bird sips honey from the flower, the yellow-bird describes graceful geometric curves in her flight. Unity in variety, gracefulness, harmony, utility every where! Beautiful colors, beautiful forms, beautiful sounds, beautiful motions the world over! Nature ever moves in lines of beauty. "Beauty is the moment of transition, as if the form were just ready to flow into other forms." The ocean of beauty in which the world swims to-day is such as was never seen before, nor shall be seen again. With each moment all is changed and all is new.

Beauty is an expression of God's thought. In its presence a feeling akin to that of worship possesses the soul. There is recognized a beauty far deeper than that which we see—unexplored and unexplorable. What is visible is but the veil which conceals beauty, or through which beauty dimly shines. The most beautiful object is that from which the divine looks most freely.

There is a boundless and fathomless sea. We gaze and lose ourselves—enjoyment is at its height. It is something within an object which makes it beautiful.

The highest kind of beauty belongs to man. Emerson says: "Every spirit makes its home; and we can give a shrewd guess from the house to the inhabitant. But not less does nature furnish us with every sign of grace and goodness. The delicious faces of children, the beauty of school-girls, 'the sweet seriousness of sixteen,' the lofty air of well-born, well-bred boys, the passionate histories in the looks and manners of youth and early manhood, and the varied power in all that well-known company that escort us through life—we know how these forms thrill, paralyze, provoke, inspire, and enlarge us" The loveliness of the human form reaches its height in woman. "To Eve," say the Mohammedans, "God gave two thirds of all beauty," and it has not become less among her daughters. The virtuous and accomplished Pauline de Viguiere, of Toulouse, was so enchanting in her loveliness that she quite intoxicated her native city. When she appeared on the balcony twice a week, at the command of the civil authorities, the throng who came to behold her beauty was so great as to endanger life. Walpole says: "The concourse was so great when the Duchess of Hamilton was presented to court, on Friday, that even the noble crowd in the drawing-room clambered on chairs and tables to look at her. There are mobs at their doors to see them get into their chairs, and people go early to get places at the theaters when it is known they will be there." Elsewhere he says: "Such crowds flock to see the Duchess of Hamilton that seven hundred people sat up all night, in and about an inn, in Yorkshire, to see her get into her post-chaise next morning."

Beauty may become a dangerous possession. Cleopatra was at once the most beautiful and the wickedest of queens. We have little admiration for Judith. Beauty, when sustained by character, thought, and heart, is priceless. Mere beauty of person charms no longer when we miss moral beauty, while an ugly face becomes positively quite tolerable when we discover a pure soul *behind* the face. "There are faces so fluid with expression, so flushed and rippled by the play of thought, that we can hardly find what the mere features really are." Character throws an immortal splendor about a soul. The pure shall shine as stars. A beautiful soul gathers beauties as it passes through the world.

So far as beauty is not spiritual, so far as it has not its permanent home in the heart and thought of God, it is fleeting indeed. All visible forms are short-lived; the sweetest songs die in the singing. Yet we instinctively recognize true beauty as immortal. Whenever a beautiful form or a beautiful thought is created the world adopts it, locks it up in memory, multiplies it, immortalizes it. The beautiful is spiritual and everlasting. All language recognizes this truth. When we use the word beauty with reference to the invisible and immaterial, we may, after all, be using words in the most just sense. We speak of the beauty of the adaptation of means to an end, the beauty of a mathematical demonstration, a beautiful experiment, a beautiful poem, a beautiful act, a beautiful thought, a beautiful life, a beautiful death. Such beauty abides forever. There are beauties quite near which are immeasurable and divine. It is a part of that which enspheres the earth and bejewels the sky. All faces and forms would be beautiful had lives been always pure. As it is, a face is a sculptured history, in which, as Emerson says, there are many chapters of foibles, follies, and sins. The art of beauty is to live a beautiful life, to bid the Holy Spirit welcome to come in and beautify his own temple and there abide.

"Esther, in addition to her outward comeliness, was modest, engaging, contented, and possessed all those amiable qualities which adorn the individual, while they make him useful to society. Beauty is one of the gifts of nature; but if it consist only in symmetry of form and fineness of coloring, it is no more than a beautiful statue; it can only gratify the eye." *

We are quite prepared, then, to learn that "when

* McCrie.

the king's commandment and his decree was heard, and when many maidens were gathered together unto Shushan the palace, to the custody of Hegai, Esther was brought also unto the king's house to the custody of Hegai, keeper of the women." By her gracefulness of person and movement, beauty of face, queenly dignity, and modesty of demeanor, she quickly won the favor of Hegai, who did not fail to advance her interests.

"He speedily gave her things for purification," that she might be among the first to be presented to the great king. Exod. xxx, 23-25; Prov. vii, 17. And he furnished her "such things as belonged to her," or food best adapted to the development of both health and beauty. To each virgin he gave seven maidens from the king's service to keep her company and do her bidding, but the maidens which he assigned Esther were seven *picked maidens*. To complete the furnishment of his favorite he selected for her use the finest suite of rooms at his command in the whole palace.

Esther, in obedience to the suggestion of Mordecai, "had not showed her people nor her kindred." Her kindred may have been kept a secret for prudential reasons, for, had her nationality been known, perhaps she would not have been chosen for the royal harem. It will be remembered that the king, according to law, could take a wife from but seven of the leading families of Persia. Mordecai may have shrewdly judged that, were her Jewish extraction known, her hopes of royal favor would have been blasted. In this, however, he would have forgotten the supremacy of despotic will.

Herodotus relates the following account of the marriage of Cambyses: "It was not the custom of the Persians, before his time, to marry their sisters—but Cambyses, happening to fall in love with one of his, and wishing to take her to wife, as he knew that it was an uncommon thing, called together the royal judges, and put it to them, 'whether there was any law which allowed a brother, if he wished, to marry his sister?' Now the royal judges are certain picked men among the Persians, who hold their office for life, or until they are found guilty of some misconduct. By them justice is administered in Persia, and they are the interpreters of the old laws, all disputes being referred to their decision. When Cambyses, therefore, put his question to these judges, they gave him an answer which was at once true and safe—'they did not find any law,' they said, 'allowing a brother to take his sister to wife, but they found a law, that the king of the Persians might do what he pleased.' And so they neither warped the law through fear of Cambyses, nor ruined themselves by over stiffly maintaining the law; but they brought another quite distinct law to the king's help, which allowed him to have his wish. Cambyses, therefore, married the object of his love, and no long time afterward he took to wife another sister. It was the younger of these who went with him into Egypt, and there suffered death at his hands." *

Artaxerxes Memnon married two of his own daughters. In Egypt brother and sister might marry, and in the age of the patriarchs a man might marry his half sister. Gen. xx, 12. Xerxes, then, would not have found the law an insuperable objection to his marriage with the Jewish maiden. Mordecai may not have known the ease with which a Persian king could circumvent the law "which changeth not."

"And Mordecai walked every day before the court of the women's house to know how Esther did, and what should become of her."

"Mordecai occupied, apparently, an humble place in the royal household. He was probably one of the porters or door-keepers at the main entrance of the palace. See ver. 21, and comp. chap. iii, 2; v. 13, etc. His position separated him from his adopted daughter, and some effort was needed to keep up communication with her." †

He "walked" up and down every day. "Mordecai's fatherly care is beautiful; equaled only by Esther's filial affection and obedience." ‡

* Herodotus, iii, 31.   † Rawlinson.   ‡ Greene.

"Indeed, *every day* hardly does justice to the double emphasis of the original in its expression of Mordecai's intense anxiety." *

In this life of the beautiful Jewish maiden, which is now opening to our study, we behold the complete consecration of personal qualities to God and his cause. Among the talents with which she was endowed may be reckoned her personal beauty. This she counted sacred to the service of her divine king. Every power of mind, every affection of heart, every moral quality, every advantage of social position, every material possession, and every personal attraction are so many talents to be used for God's glory.

Esther was ever obedient to the calls and indications of Providence. The great man is the man who recognizes providences, yields to the voices which command from the unseen world, and seizes opportunities as they pass. He it is who ever strives to keep near the heart of God. Only the loving and loyal soul can God effectively use as an instrument for the accomplishment of his purposes. Only such a soul lives in harmony with himself, his surroundings, and his God. He falls naturally into God's plan, and, like every creature in its appropriate place, is omnipotent within his sphere. Esther was passive in God's hands to be directed, and active and prompt to obey the will of her Father in heaven.

* Alcott.

The law of providential systems is easily discoverable in this history. Around the Israelitish nation as a central sun there revolved, with greater or less regularity, the planets of God's providences. Every thing had reference to this central body. It gave out its light to enlighten surrounding peoples; they in turn worked out God's designs. Wars, revolutions, discoveries, centuries, great men, national calamities, natural catastrophies—all, controlled by the Omnipotent Hand, worked together for the good of this central sun. God never lost sight of his own people. Their exile, which threatened destruction to the race, proved a blessing: the heathen influences which surrounded them drove the remnant nearer to God.

Providential systems revolve around the individual who is loyal to the cause of righteousness. God sees the *ones*. All things work together for the good of the ones. Things are done as they are in this world with reference to the chosen of God. Israel is safe as a nation so long as it is loyal to Jehovah. Esther is safe in the land of her exile so long as she is true to the God of her fathers. God found her, recognized her worth, and placed her on a throne. She was now in a position to help her people. So ever work God's providences. The world is governed to serve spiritual ends. Each loyal soul is a center around which numberless providences revolve. These providences work together for the true interests of the soul.

The Christian to-day is watched over, guarded, defended, and delivered. All things are his. He is ensphered in the Lord, and no harm can touch his soul. There are no favorites in God's kingdom. Every daughter of Christ is as dear to him as was Esther; and every believer in Christ is a prince of the blood. The kingdoms of to-day are ruled by the Omnipotent for the advancement of his cause and the good of his people.

CHAPTER VII.

ENTHRONED AND CROWNED.

"And the king loved Esther above all the women, and she obtained grace and favor in his sight more than all the virgins; so that he set the royal crown upon her head, and made her queen instead of Vashti."—ESTHER ii, 17.

ESTHER was now in the palace of the great king. Her food was the choicest which the king's bounty could supply; she occupied the most spacious and the most elegantly furnished and at the same time the pleasantest suite of apartments in all "the king's house," and seven maidens rare of beauty and accomplishments waited to do her bidding while she enjoyed the special favoritism of Hegai, "the king's chamberlain."

Twelve months preparation were necessary before she could be presented to the king. During this time she was put to the strictest diet and discipline of purification. Luxurious baths were provided with costliest perfumes and unguents. "Six months with oil of myrrh, and six months with sweet odors, and with *other* things" were appointed for her purification "according to the manner of the women." All this was done to insure perfect health of body, the greatest beauty of face and symmetry of form, and smoothness and softness of skin.

The art of beauty among Oriental nations was a most important study. The eyes, the teeth, the lips, the hair, the nails, the arms—the whole body was studied, beautified and adorned.

ARTICLES FOR THE TOILET.

Lane describes the process of coloring the eyelids among the Egyptians: "The eyes, with very few exceptions, are black, large, and of a long almond form, with long and beautiful lashes, and an exquisitely soft, bewitching expression; eyes more beautiful can hardly be conceived; their charming effect is much heightened by the concealment of the other features (however pleasing the latter may be), and is rendered still more striking by a practice universal among the females of the higher and middle classes, and very common among those of the lower orders, which is that of blackening the edge of the eye-lids, both above and below the eyes, with a black powder called *kohl*. This is a collyrium, commonly composed of the smoke-black which is produced by burning a kind of *libám*—an aromatic resin—a species of frankincense, used, I am told, in preference to the better kind of frankincense, as being cheaper, and equally good for the purpose. Kohl is also prepared of the smoke-black produced from burning the shells of almonds. These two kinds, though believed to be beneficial to the eyes, are used merely for ornament; but there are several kinds used for their real or supposed medicinal properties, particularly the powder of several kinds of lead ore, to which are often added sarcocolla, long pepper, sugar-candy, fine dust of Venetian squim, and sometimes powdered pearls. Antimony, it is said, was formerly used for painting the edges of the eyelids. The kohl is applied with a small probe of wood, ivory, or silver, tapering toward the end, but blunt; this is moistened sometimes with rose-water, then dipped in the powder and drawn along the edges of the eyelids."

The sculptures and paintings on temples and tombs show the prevalence of this custom among both sexes in most ancient times. The kohl bottles, still containing some of the paint and the bodkins for applying it, have been found, after a burial of thousands of years.

Painting the eyes is mentioned in the Scriptures. It prevailed also among the ladies of Greece.

The number, variety, and weight of the ornaments worn by the Orientals were most extravagant, as measured by modern western ideas. The ladies of ancient Egypt wore earrings of great size, and bracelets, armlets, and anklets of the most varied character. These ornaments were frequently richly inlaid with enamel or precious stones. Handsome and costly gold or bead necklaces were highly esteemed. The modern Egyptians vie with the ancients in the number, variety, beauty, and value of their ornaments. "Most of the women of the lower orders wear a variety of trumpery ornaments," thus rivaling the rich and noble in their desire for display.

EAR-DROPS.

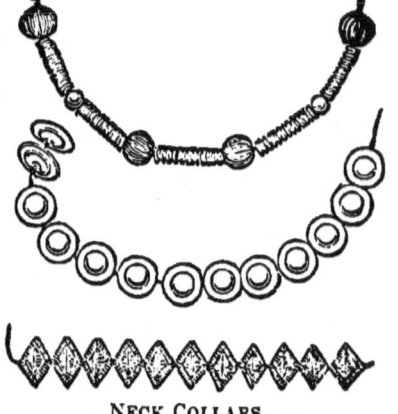
NECK COLLARS.

The inhabitants of Palestine and the surrounding countries were equally fond of personal adornment. Earrings, nose-rings, bracelets, signets, gold neck-chains, and trinkets of various kinds, both of gold and of silver, were abundant. Such ornaments supplied the gold from which were made the sacred utensils of the tabernacle. The laver of brass was constructed from the brazen mirrors of the women's toilet. The Israelites gathered from the slain Midianites ornaments to the amount of sixteen thousand seven hundred and fifty shekels; and again, after the defeat of the same people by Gideon, there were obtained nose-rings to the amount of one thousand and seven hundred shekels of gold, besides collars and earrings.

The love of ornament is rebuked by Isaiah: "In that day the Lord will take away the bravery of their anklets, and the cauls, and the crescents; the pendants, and the bracelets, and the mufflers; the head-tires, and the ankle chains, and the sashes, and the perfume boxes, and the amulets; the rings, and the nose jewels; the festival robes, and the mantels, and the shawls, and the satchels; the hand mirrors, and the fine linen, and the turbans, and the veils." Isa. iii, 18–23. The ankle chains gave the mincing walk supposed to characterize the nobility.

The Mishna, in speaking of proper articles of dress and announcing its law, says: "A woman must not go out (on the Sabbath) with linen or woolen laces, nor with the straps on her head: nor with a frontlet and pendants thereto, unless sown to her cap: nor with a golden tower (that is, an ornament in the shape of a tower): nor with a tight gold chain: nor with nose-rings: nor with finger rings on which there is no seal: nor with a needle without an eye: nor with a finger ring that has a seal on it: nor with a diadem: nor with a smelling bottle or balm flask." A man may go out with knee-buckles, but not with an amulet, nor a step-chain. There was much reason for the apostle Paul's recommending the women to adorn themselves "not with braided hair, or gold, or pearls, or costly array, but with good works," and with "the ornament of a meek and quiet spirit, which is in the sight of God of great price." Ornaments were most lavishly displayed especially at festivals, when every lady was desirous of appearing at her best.

The early Chaldean women wore bronze and iron bangles and amulets, and bracelets of rings or beads; also earrings and rings for the toes. These various rings were shell, bronze, or iron. Strings of gold and agate beads surrounded the neck. The men wore seal-cylinders of agate or other hard stone, and sometimes rings and bracelets, the last being occasionally of gold.

The Assyrians and Babylonians were also doubtless given to extravagant personal adornment, though the monuments afford meager information on this point. The Persians, when the great empire was at the height of its magnificence, lavished upon themselves richest jewelry and most gorgeous attire. The cus-

ENTHRONED AND CROWNED. 135

tom of using dyes to enhance the brilliancy of the eyes, and give them greater apparent size and softness, was borrowed by the Persians from the Medes.

After all possible care, few were the fortunate concubines who were called the second time to the king's apartments. "Now when every maid's turn came to go into King Ahasuerus,* in the evening she went, and on the morrow she returned into the second house of the women, to the custody of Shaashgaz, the king's chamberlain, which kept the king's concubines. She came in unto the king no more, except the king delighted in her, and that she were called by name." It is not a matter for wonder that each maid used every art to enhance her beauty, and that "whatever she desired" of ornaments and jewelry were given her by Hegai.

"Now when the turn of Esther, the daughter of Abihail, the uncle of Mordecai, who had taken her for his daughter, was come to go in unto the king, she required nothing but what Hegai, the king's chamberlain, the keeper of the women, appointed." This was quite different from the choice of the other virgins.

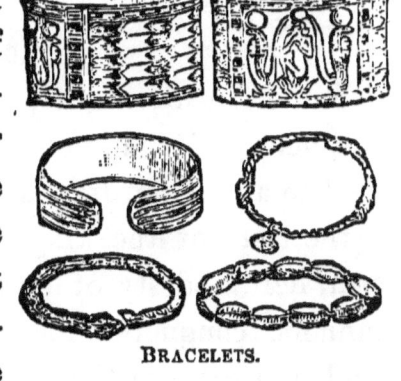

BRACELETS.

* Herodotus refers to the custom in iii, 69.

"No doubt the virgins generally took the opportunity—one that would occur but once in their lives—to load themselves with precious ornaments of various kinds, necklaces, bracelets, ear-rings, anklets, and the like. Esther allowed Hegai to dress her as he would."*

"Not, perhaps, because of shrewdness, as if she depended on the fact that Hegai understood best the taste of the king; she did not design to please the king by means of ornamentation, and only put on what was deemed indispensable by Hegai." †

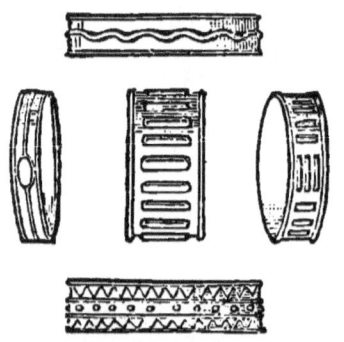
ARMLETS.

"Thus, as ever, it proves that true piety is the highest ornament, even in a heathen's sight, and modesty is the brightest jewel of female beauty." 1 Pet. iii, 3, 4.‡

There was certainly no intentional shrewdness on the part of Esther in leaving her personal adornment to the judgment of Hegai, yet doubtless she was thereby enabled to appear in dress and ornaments most pleasing to the taste of the king. Her beauty of face and form, her modesty of dress, and her gracefulness of manners, conquered his heart. The riches of her mind and the affections of her gentle heart, her discretion, dutifulness, and integrity, and all fair qualities, adorned her pure life.

* Rawlinson. † Schultz. ‡ Strong.

The preparation which Esther made when called to enter the presence of the king met with the commendation of all who knew her. "And Esther obtained favor in the sight of all them that looked upon her."

At length she was ushered into the apartments of her royal lord. It was in the month Tebeth, four years after the divorce of Vashti. The ancient Chaldeans named the month Tebit, "the month of the cave of the rising sun," the month in which the ancients celebrated the birth of the new sun after his death and concealment amid the fogs and storms of "the month of thick clouds," or Kislev. It corresponds with December-January, in which Christians celebrate the birth of the Sun of Righteousness. In this month, then, the Myrtle of Israel went into the house royal, and in this month the star of the exile shone forth. The king was enamored of the beautiful Jewish maiden at the first. Mordecai, whose anxiety was deep and tender, could rejoice in the fortunes of his fair cousin. "The king loved Esther above all the women, and she obtained grace and favor in his sight more than all the virgins; so that he set the royal crown upon her head, and made her queen instead of Vashti."

The wedding was celebrated with a magnificence commensurate with the greatness, the wealth, and the glory of the kingdom. As a special honor to the successful favorite, the feast was called "Esther's feast." Princes, embassadors, nobles, conquerors, and all great men were present. The king, as ever, was proud and haughty, while Esther, dazzling all with her beauty, charming all with her modesty and grace, and captivating all by her noble and yet gentle bearing, walked a queen.

It was the custom of Persian kings to dispense royal favors and bounties with an open hand upon all great occasions. The subjects of Pseudo-Smerdis, "while his reign lasted, received great benefits from him, insomuch that, when he died, all the dwellers in Asia mourned his loss exceedingly, except only the Persians. For no sooner did he come to the throne than forthwith he sent round to every nation under his rule and granted them freedom from war-service and from taxes for the space of three years."* Speaking of the Lacedæmonians, Herodotus says: "They hold with the Persians: when the king dies and another comes to the throne, the newly-made monarch forgives all the Spartans the debts they owe, either to the king or to the public treasury. And, in like manner among the Persians, each king, when he begins to reign, remits the tribute due from the provinces."†

So upon this joyous occasion Xerxes "made a release to the provinces." He also "gave gifts," and these gifts were "according to the state of the king,"

---

* Herodotus, iii, 6, 7. † Ibid. vi, 59.

gifts that became "the honor of his excellent majesty."

Persian kings bestowed on their queens and other favorites villages and cities, to supply them with articles of food, dress, and other conveniences and luxuries. Certain villages of Syria were given to Parysatis to furnish her with girdles. Anthylla, in Egypt, under Persian rule, was assigned to the wife of the ruler of Egypt, to keep her in shoes.*

Socrates says: "I have been informed by a credible person who went up to the king (at Susa) that he passed through a large tract of excellent land, extending for nearly a day's journey, which the people of the country called 'the queen's girdle,' and another which they called her 'veil,' and several other fair and fertile districts, which were reserved for the adornment of the queen, and are named after her several habiliments." †

According to Diodorus, the revenues of Lake Moeris were settled on the Queen of Egypt, to supply her with ointments, jewels, and other articles connected with her toilet.

In like manner Esther and other favorites of the king were royally remembered on this day of happy auspices, and the fair queen doubtless more than all the rest.

* Xenophon, *Anabasis* I. iv, 8; Herodotus, ii, 98.
† Plato, *Alcibiades* I. 123.

There is another gathering of virgins to replenish the royal harem. Mordecai at this time fills some office at "the king's gate." The queen has not forgotten her noble cousin and benefactor. "Esther had not yet showed her kindred nor her people, as Mordecai had charged her: for Esther did the commandment of Mordecai, like as when she was brought up with him." Esther ii, 20.

"We have here a daughter bereft of the protection of man by the death of her parents, but God elevated her to great distinction, so that all men gave her honor. Why was she carried into exile, but that she should reign? Why bereft of parents, unless that she might become the favorite of God and man?"[*]

[*] Brenz.

VIII.

THE CONSPIRACY DISCOVERED.

"Two of the king's chamberlains . . . sought to lay hand on the king."—ESTHER ii, 21.

"The thing was known to Mordecai, who told it unto Esther."—ESTHER ii, 22.

"They were both hanged on a tree: and it was written in the book of the chronicles before the king."—ESTHER ii, 23.

TROUBLES multiplied in the palace of the king. The sins and excesses which marked his career began to bear their legitimate fruit. Among the king's chamberlains were two men honored with positions near the royal person, and implicitly trusted. These were Bigthan or Bigtha, whose name, of good omen, has been derived from the old Persian *Bagadana*, "the God-given," and Teresh, whose name, of doubtful omen, may possibly be derived from *tars*, "to fear." Through anger, or jealousy, or for some other cause, they formed a secret plot to assassinate the king, but Mordecai, who also held some position at the king's gate, discovered the conspiracy and reported it to the queen, who at once informed Xerxes. The conspirators were apprehended, tried, found guilty, and condemned to death.

Such conspiracies inside the palace were frequent

occurrences in Persia. Xerxes, though escaping from this and doubtless other plots, was ultimately murdered by Artabanus, captain of his guard, and Aspamistras, a chamberlain. Artaxerxes Ochus met the same fate.

The criminals were hurried away to execution. Various methods of execution are mentioned in the Scriptures, of which the most usual were stoning to death, and slaying with the sword or with an ax. Executions by means of saws and harrows of iron, and by forcing the criminal through a brick-kiln, were exceptional and barbarous.

Bigthan and Teresh were executed by "impalement." "The punishment inflicted by Xerxes succeeded those with which the Assyrians and the Babylonians and the eastern nations generally were familiar. These are exhibited on the marbles and bronzes that have been exhumed from the mounds of Assyria. There has not yet been shown any example of hanging by the neck, or of fastening to a cross. There are abundant examples of impalement, of which the most ancient, those of the Balowat gates (850 B.C), shows the impalement to have been" by passing the stake through the body along the spine, sometimes the entire length of the body. "The method of accomplishing this in modern times, as practiced by the Khan of Khiva, has been to make use of two carriages, binding the victim to the one, and securing the stake to the other, and thus readily applying any amount of force that might be required. In some instances cords were bound around the legs of the victim, and thus he was drawn down upon the stake. Instances of impalement by the Turks of Bosnia are given on the best authority as late as 1876."

In connection with the illustrations of the most ancient impalement "are shown the barbarous amputation of hands and feet, and the impalement of heads. A little later we find numerous impalements from below the breast. One slab shows us three of these, another fourteen. Darius is said to have impaled three thousand of the nobility of Babylon when he took that city."

"If we would read the Old Testament aright, we must understand every case of hanging on a tree, except that of Absalom (caught by his hair) as denoting impalement on a stake, instead of suspension by a halter." *

Thus the conspirators were slain, and the king, according to his custom, caused the name of Mordecai to be recorded among his benefactors.

When the great and mighty host of Xerxes was marshaled for the invasion of Greece, the king reviewed his army and fleet. Herodotus gives the following account: "Accordingly he traversed the

---

* The Lowell Hebrew Club, The Book of Esther, pp. 126, 127, 130; Herodotus, iv, 43; iii, 125, 159; Ezra, vi, 11.

ranks, seated in his chariot, and going from nation to nation made manifold inquiries, while his scribes wrote down the answers; till at last he had passed from end to end of the whole land army, both the horsemen and likewise the foot. This done he exchanged his chariot for a Sidonian galley, and, seated beneath a golden awning, sailed along the prows of all his vessels (the vessels having now been hauled down and launched into the sea), while he made inquiries again, as he had done when he reviewed the land-forces, and caused the answers to be recorded by his scribes."

At the battle of Salamis the king observed carefully the conduct of his troops, "and whenever he saw any of his own captains perform any worthy exploit, he inquired concerning him; and the man's name was taken down by his scribes, together with the names of his father and his city." Phylacus, who took a vessel from the Greeks in this great battle, in recognition of this heroic action was enrolled by Xerxes among the "king's benefactors."

The Persians called the king's benefactors *Orosangs*, which may mean "those worthy of being recorded." The inscriptions of Assyria and Babylonia repeatedly speak of "recording the name" as the highest honor. The right to have such record made belonged exclusively to the king. Josephus mentions this custom, and Thucydides is an authority for its use in Persia.

Pausanius, the Spartan commander, prosecuting an intrigue with the king, restored certain captives, whereupon Xerxes replied: "Thus saith Xerxes, the king, to Pausanius. The benefit which thou hast done me, in saving the captives who were taken at Byzantium beyond the sea, is recorded in my house forever." *

These records are made by direction of the king, but probably not by his own hand. He may never have consulted a book, nor studied any branch of learning, and hence would have been incompetent even to record his own edicts. It is quite probable that he would consider such work beneath his kingly dignity. To pass away his time a scribe sometimes read to him from the chronicles of the kings, but he took no further interest in these matters. The court scribe wrote the letters, edicts and inscriptions. The king held councils, reviewed troops, heard complaints, rendered decisons, tried causes when not delegated to "royal judges," distributed rewards and punishments, directed the civil administration, led the armies to battle, listened to reports concerning the condition of affairs in the different provinces of the realm, and issued necessary commands. The burden of government, however, was frequently placed upon some favorite. Much of the attention of the king

* Herodotus, vii, 100; viii, 85, 90; iii, 140; Josephus, *Antiquities*, xi, 6; Thucydides, i, 129; Diodorous, xvii, 14; Aelian, Hist. Var. 40.

10

was directed to the preparation of his own tomb. In his leisure moments he sometimes played dice, carved wood or hunted in his paradises.

The name of Mordecai, then, by direction of the king, was enrolled among the king's benefactors in "the book of the chronicles." Ctesias claims to have had access to these royal archives in the preparation of his history. They are mentioned in certain books of the Old Testament, and the authors of these books seem to have drawn from such records portions of the material which is woven into their histories.

IX.

PRIDE BEFORE A FALL.

"And all the king's servants, that were in the king's gate, bowed, and reverenced Haman."—ESTHER iii, 2.

"But Mordecai bowed not, nor did him reverence."—ESTHER iii, 2.

THE early Amalekites were a powerful and fierce people who dwelt in Arabia-Petræa, between Havilah and Shur, or between the Dead Sea and the Red Sea. They were defeated by Chedorlaomer, King of Elam, in the days of Abraham. According to Arabian historians, their original home was on the Persian Gulf. The Assyrians pressed upon them, and, yielding before this rising power, they spread over a portion of Arabia before its settlement by the Joktanites. The presence of the names "Amalek," "the mount of the Amalekites," and "the tombs of the Amalekites," indicates a permanent occupation of Central Palestine in their migration westward. The oldest Arab traditions make the Amalika descendants from Aram and Lud —the Hamite Lud, son of Mizraim, called in the Egyptian language "Lut" or "Rut." If this tradition be accepted as historic, they were a mixed race of Aramæn and Egyptian blood, uniting Shem and Ham.

The Amalika drove out the Amu from Arabia-Petræa, where they had dwelt since the third and fourth Egyptian dynasties, and pushed them back to the mountain chain of Sinai. The ancestors of the Amalekites may have been the Herusha, and perhaps also the Shasu, with whom Egypt contended in the early dynasties. "The Saāru of the tribes of Shasu," conquered by Rameses III., Brugsch Bey identifies with the Seirites, a cave-dwelling people in the ridges and concealed places of the wildest mountains.

It will be remembered that the names of ancient peoples are frequently quite flexible in the geographical and ethnographical denotations. The name *Amalika* may have been used to designate several different tribes.

When Esau fled to Mount Seir, his grandson, Amalek, settled in the midst of the Amalekites, and possibly became the founder of the royal family. This fierce race was the first to make war against the Hebrews upon their deliverance from the bondage of Egypt. They seem at that time to have occupied the whole of the northern part of the peninsula—a wild region, suited to a wild race; educating them to freedom, endurance, love of the chase, and war. There they led a roving life, ranging at will amid wildest scenery, over rugged passes and under high cliffs, through gigantic forms and virgin forests, where nature is still fresh from the hand of God. They are "the first of the nations," under the leadership of a king who bore the hereditary name of Agag, "the fiery."

The battle took place at Rephidim, "the place of rest," the first great halting place, now the valley of Paran. Joshua, the Ephraimite, with a chosen army met the enemy on the field, while Moses, the leader, Aaron, his brother, and Hur, of the tribe of Judah, Moses's brother-in-law, the husband of the prophetess Miriam, went up to the top of the hill to beseech the help of God. "And it came to pass, when Moses held up his hand, that Israel prevailed: and when he let down his hand, Amalek prevailed. But Moses's hands were heavy, and they took a stone, and put it under him, and he sat thereon; and Aaron and Hur stayed up his hands, the one on the one side, and the other on the other side; and his hands were steady until the going down of the sun. And Joshua discomfited Amalek and his people with the edge of the sword." Exod. xvii, 11-13.

From thenceforth there was deadly hatred between the two nations, and the Amalekites, as the first of heathen nations, were doomed to utter destruction. Because their hand was against the Lord, therefore he will have war with Amalek "from generation to generation." Exod. xvii, 16; 1 Sam. xv, 2, 3; Num. xxiv, 20.

The Amalekites formed an alliance with the Canaanites and defeated the Israelites at Hormah. During the period of the judges they were ever in league with the enemies of Israel. With the Moabites they were defeated by Ehud near Jericho. With the Midianites they were defeated by Gideon in the plain of Esdraelon. By command of Samuel, Saul made war against them, overran their country, overwhelmingly defeated them, took the "city of Amalek," and made their king Agag prisoner. This reduced them to "a horde of banditti," but though few in numbers they still thirsted for the blood of Israel. A "troop" came to Ziklag, pillaged the town, and carried off a number of prisoners, among whom were Ahinoam and Abigail, wives of David, to whom the town had been assigned as a residence by Achish, the Phœnician king. David, upon his return home, learned of the calamity, pursued, overtook, and smote them, killing all save four hundred who rode "upon camels and fled." We do not hear of the Amalekites after the time of David, for the "Amalekites" spoken of at a later period seem to have belonged to another race.

From this general slaughter of the nation there had escaped one Haman, who might have been of royal blood and hence was called "the Agagite." "The name Haman is probably the same which is found in the classical writers under the form of Omanes, and which in ancient Persian would have been *Umana* or *Umanish,* an exact equivalent of the Greek 'Eumenes.' Hammedatha is perhaps the same as

Madâta or Mahadâta,* an Old Persian name signifying 'given by (or to) the moon.'" †

If Haman is not a natural descendant of the Amalekites, he is certainly their spiritual descendant, and hence a true Agagite and an enemy of the Jews.

This Haman acquired great influence at the Persian court, and was at last raised to the office of Prime Minister. A distinguished honor was bestowed upon him when the king commanded all his servants to prostrate themselves before him as the representative of his own royalty, and in recognition of his divine character.

When the six conspirators saw the omens which designated Darius as king, "it seemed as if the heavens conspired with Darius, and hereby inaugurated him king; so the five other nobles leaped with one accord from their steeds, and bowed down before him and owned him for their king."‡

The Persian king was recognized as a divinity. Æschylus, in "The Persians," makes the "Chorus of Aged Persians" call: "But do thou, O Earth, and ye other rulers of the infernal regions, suffer the illustrious divinity, the god of the Persians, born in Susa, to pass from your dwellings, and send him into upper air, such an one as never heretofore Persian mold covered. Ay, dear was the man, and dear is his

---

* Madates of Q. Curtius.   † Rawlinson.   ‡ Herodotus, iii, 86.

sepulcher, for dear was the character that it entombs. And thou, Aïdoneus, that dost send the shades to this upper world, set at liberty, Aïdoneus, Darius, all kingly as he was. Alas! For as at no time he was the destroyer of men by the wasting calamities of war, so he was called by his Persians, counselor divine; and counselor divine he was, for he conducted the host well. Lord, ancient lord, come, draw nigh, appear on the topmost peak of the mount, raising the saffron-dyed sandal of thy foot, displaying the crest of thy royal tiara. Come forth, O Darius, author of no ill: Hoa! Show thyself, sovereign lord, that thou mayest hear the sorrows of our sovereign, strange in their nature, and new."*

When the embassy of the Lacedæmonians came into the presence of Xerxes they were excused from bowing, for thereby they would have recognized him as a god. "And afterward," history relates, "when they came to Susa into the king's presence, and the guards ordered them to fall down and do obeisance, and went so far as to use force to compel them, they refused, and said they would never do any such thing, even were their heads thrust down to the ground, for it was not their custom to worship men, and they had not come to Persia for that purpose. So they fought off the ceremony." †

---

* *The Tragedies of Æschylus*, Harper's Edition, pp. 83, 84.
† Herodotus, vii, 136.

Curtius says: "The Persians, not only out of devotion, but also from motives of policy, reverenced their kings as gods, for majesty is the safeguard of the empire."*

Prostrations before officers of rank inferior to the king were common. "When they meet each other in the streets you may know if the persons meeting are of equal rank by the following token: if they are, instead of speaking, they kiss each other on the lips. In the case where one is a little inferior to the other the kiss is given on the cheek; where the difference of rank is great the inferior prostrates himself upon the ground."† Such prostrations were familiar to the Jews, and were sanctified by the example of the fathers. Gen. xxiii, 12; xlii, 6; 2 Sam. xiv, 4; 1 Kings i, 16.

The prostrations required by Xerxes must have been something more than the ordinary courtesies due to the office. No special command would have been required to enforce such courtesies. It is entirely consistent with the character of Xerxes to have arrogated to himself full divine honors and to have required worshipful recognition of his chief representative on the part of all subordinates.

We are not surprised to learn that when "all the king's servants, that were in the king's gate, bowed, and reverenced Haman," "Mordecai bowed not, nor

---

* Herodotus, viii, 5, 11. † *Ibid.*, i, 134.

did him reverence." It was not from lack of loyalty to the king's government and the king's person. He had already saved the life of his royal master and was doubtless a faithful servant. It was not from

ORIENTAL PROSTRATION.

lack of respect for the office and for the officer as such. Nehemiah and Ezra, both earnest Jews, found no difficulty in serving the great king, and bowed themselves before him as did the Persians. It was not because he did not recognize the king's command as imperative. He knew that to disobey it would peril his life. None but the weightiest reasons could have led him to disobedience. He was called upon to render to a human being that worship which was due to God alone, and to reverence him whom, as an Agagite, God had cursed.

Haman was so proud in the enjoyment of his newly-acquired honors that for some time he did not notice the disobedience of Mordecai. His attention is probably first called to it by his servants, who have doubtless once and again spoken to the Jew concerning his disregard of the royal will. Mordecai has told them that his religion prevents this act of worship.

The Talmud has the following account: "The servants of the king's gate said to Mordecai, 'Why wilt thou refuse to bow before Haman, transgressing thus the wishes of the king? Do we not bow before him?'

"'Ye are foolish,' answered Mordecai; 'aye, wanting in reason. Listen to me. Shall a mortal, who must return to dust, be glorified? Shall I bow down before one born of woman, whose days are short? When he is small he cries and weeps as a child; when he grows older sorrow and sighing are his portion; his days are full of wrath and anger, and at the end he returns to dust. Shall I bow to one like him? No, I prostrate myself before the Eternal God, who lives forever; who dwells in heaven and bears the world in the hollow of his hand. His word changes sunlight to darkness, his command illumines the deepest gloom. His wisdom made the world, he placed the boundaries of the mighty sea; the waters are his, the sweet and the salt; to the struggling waves he says, 'Be still; thus far shalt thou come, no further, that the earth may remain dry for my people.' To him, the great Creator and Ruler of the Universe, and to no other will I bow."*

Vashti dared the wrath of the king and was divorced. Daniel disobeyed a similar command and was cast into the den of lions. The three Hebrews disobeyed and were cast into the burning furnace. The servants of the king, having reported the disobe-

* Polano, *Selections from the Talmud*, pp. 191, 192.

dience of Mordecai to Haman, wait to see if his excuse will be accepted as sufficient. To be sure the Lacedæmonian embassadors were excused for the same reason which Mordecai has urged, but the circumstances in many respects were quite different. What will be done to Mordecai the Jew?

CHAPTER X.

SUPERSTITION AND CRUELTY, HAND IN HAND.

Then was Haman full of wrath.—ESTHER iii, 5.
Haman sought to destroy all the Jews.—ESTHER iii, 6.
Let it be written that they may be destroyed.—ESTHER iii, 9.
And the king and Haman sat down to drink; but the city Shushan was perplexed.—ESTHER iii, 15.

WHEN Haman was informed of the contumacy of Mordecai he was "full of wrath." He would not allow the fact of his Jewish nationality and religion to be an excuse for such an affront. Mordecai, indeed, was beneath his notice, and he scorned to lay hands on him alone, but he "sought to destroy all the Jews that *were* throughout the whole kingdom."

History furnishes illustrious examples of such wholesale massacre. The Scythians had overrun the richest provinces of Asia and held possession of them for some years, till "at length Cyaxares and the Medes invited the greater part of them to a banquet, and made them drunk with wine, after which they were all massacred."* When the seven conspirators assassinated Pseudo-Smerdis, the Persians began the slaughter of the magi, and "such was their fury,

* Herodotus, i, 106.

that, unless night had closed in, not a single magus would have been left alive."* Mithridates, the Parthian king, "issued orders to all the governors and cities dependent on him to put to death on one and the same day all Italians residing within their bounds, whether free or slaves, without distinction of sex or age, and on no account, under severe penalties, to aid any of the proscribed to escape; to cast forth the corpses of the slain as a prey to the birds; to confiscate their property, and to hand over one half of it to the murderers and the other half to the king. The horrible orders were—excepting in a few districts, such as the island of Cos—punctually executed, and eighty, or, according to other accounts, one hundred and fifty thousand—if not innocent, at least defenseless, men, women, and children were slaughtered in cold blood in one day in Asia Minor."†

Nothing less than the slaughter of the Jewish nation can expiate the insult offered to the Prime Minister of the empire, soothe his offended pride, and sate his vengeance. He determines upon this bloody course and makes his preparations.

He can, however, attempt nothing unless it first receive the sanction of his religion. Cruelty and superstition are ever inseparably united.

The religion of the Persians as taught by Zoroaster in the most ancient passages of the Zend-Avesta is

---

* Herod., iii, 79.   † Mommsen, *History of Rome*, vol. iii, p. 355.

one of the purest of ancient faiths, and in its earliest portions dates from about twelve hundred years before Christ.

It is most intimately connected with the religion of Moses and the prophets of the Old Testament. The magi are mentioned in the Bible, in which the Persians are not classified with idolaters. Cyrus is called " the anointed of the Lord."

The sacred books of this old religion have but lately been made accessible in modern tongues. The early religion was strictly monotheistic. Ahuramazda was the creator of all things, munificent, righteous, wise, brilliant, glorious, eternal, the essence of truth, faithful, " having his own light," " originator of all the best things of the spirit of nature, of righteousness, of the luminaries, and the self-shining brightness which is in the luminaries," giver of immortality, rewarder of good, and punisher of evil.

From this primitive monotheism was developed a dualism of good and bad spirits—God and the devil, each independent and warring against the other. The Zoroastrian believed in " the two-fold nature of man as body and soul, the two-fold origin of knowledge as heavenly and earthly, human responsibility, the value of prayer, angelic mediatorship, heaven and hell, immortality, a general judgment, future rewards and punishments according to the works, the resurrection of the body, the final overthrow of evil, and the renovation of all things." The good at death enter "the house of Song," the bad are sent to "eternal glooms."

The modern Parsi worships facing some luminous object, as best symbolizing the divine presence. His creed is, pure thoughts, pure words, and pure deeds.

Such a religion, in its purity, would not lead the Jewish exile far astray. It would strengthen in him his attachment to strict monotheism and his abhorrence of idolatry, while it would teach a pure morality and religious doctrines fundamentally correct. The spirit of evil, recognized, in its later development, as independent in origin, would not attract his worship, but would drive him closer to the good Spirit.

But he would meet with two other religions. The religion of the ancient Chaldeans was a system of nature worship highly sacerdotal in type. It was the religion of the Accadians. The priests claimed supernatural powers.

"They explained omens, expounded dreams, and by means of certain mysterious manipulations of the barsom, or bundle of twigs, arrived at a knowledge of future events, which they communicated to the pious inquirer. With such pretensions, it was natural that the caste should assume a lofty air, a stately dress, and an *entourage* of ceremonial magnificence. Clad in white robes, and bearing upon their heads tall felt caps, with long lappets at the sides, which concealed the jaw and even the lips, each with his barsom in his hand, they marched in procession to their *pyraetheia*, or fire-altars, and standing around them performed for an hour at a time their magical incantations. The credulous multitude, impressed by sights of this kind, and imposed on by the claims to supernatural power which the magi advanced, paid them a willing homage; and when the Arian tribes, pressing westward, came into contact with the races professing the Magian religion, they found a sacerdotal caste all-powerful in most of the Scythic nations." *

The classic historian says: "Scythia has an abundance of soothsayers, who foretell the future by means of a number of willow-wands. A large bundle of these rods is brought and laid on the ground. The soothsayer unties the bundle, and places each wand by itself, at the same time uttering his prophecy; then, while he is still speaking, he gathers the rods together again, and makes them up once more into a bundle." †

These wands of different lengths—consisting of some odd number—were always carried by the Magus. The baneful influence of the magi was felt by Cambyses; they became dominant and aggressive under Pseudo-Smerdis; they were massacred when the gov-

---

* Rawlinson, *Ancient Monarchies*, vol. iii, pp. 348, 349.
† Herodotus, iv, 67.

ernment was seized by Darius Hystapis; and their religion greatly modified pure Zoroastrianism, and was an influential element in the time of Xerxes.

Ezekiel speaks of divination by means of rods or arrows. Ezek. xxi, 21. The arrows of fate are represented on Babylonian cylinders as held in the hand of Marduk or Ishtar, the divinities of Jupiter and Venus, the most favorable deities, according to the Magians. A tablet in the British Museum shows a method of divination by the magic throwing of dice.*

Magical rites were multiplied. Purifications, mysteries, magic knots, magic numbers, incantations, exorcisms, sacred names and texts, talismans, amulets, charms, sorceries, witchcraft, magic spells, magic potions, imprecations, mysterious rites, powerful secrets—these were all important. Fire was worshiped, hymns were chanted, and prayers were offered. There were gods of the sea, the sky, and the storm. The sun and moon were gods, and there were many planetary divinities.

Another religion was the Semitic cult of Assyria and Babylonia, into which this elemental system was absorbed. The gods of Assyria were more clearly marked and possessed nobler attributes. Prayers and hymns showed a truer spirit of worship. But there were human sacrifices and unclean rites. Bel, Merodach, Rimmin, Nebo, Nergal, Ishtar, and Assur

* Lenormant, *Chaldean Magic*, p. 238.

were important gods. Planetary worship continued, and kings were zealous in extending their religion over conquered countries.

Many of the moral precepts were pure. Temples of worship were multiplied, and books of worship, of magic, of prayer, of praise, and of explanations were prepared. Legends concerning the creation, the flood, and other biblical events were current. The devotees of this religion believed in omens and dreams, and lucky and unlucky days. They prayed for the forgiveness of sins, sacrificed in high places, and expected future retributions. The good, they believed, went to "a place of delights," "the land of the silver sky." They had a learned priesthood, imposing ceremonies, brilliant services, magnificent temples, and many and great idols. There were many valuable fragments of truth which remained.

Xerxes found at Callatêbus a plane tree which was so beautiful that he presented it with golden ornaments and placed it under the care of one of the immortals. Ten daintily caparisoned Nisæan horses were in the army of Xerxes; also, "the holy chariot of Jupiter, drawn by eight milk-white steeds, with the charioteer on foot behind them holding the reins; for no mortal is ever allowed to mount into the car." At the Pergamus of Priam Xerxes made an offering of a thousand oxen to Minerva while the Magians poured out libations to the heroes slain at Troy. The

Strymon was propitiated by sacrificing white horses; and at "The Nine Ways" nine youths and nine maidens were buried alive.*

Strabo says that at the sacrifice to a stream "the flesh of the victim is then placed on myrtle or laurel branches; the magi touch it with slender twigs, and make incantations, pouring oil mixed with milk and honey, not into the fire, nor into the water, but upon the earth."†

Herodotus had heard that Amestris, the wife of Xerxes, "in her old age buried alive seven pairs of Persian youths, sons of illustrious men, as a thank-offering to the god who is supposed to dwell underneath the earth." The Persians sacrificed the first Greek prisoner. In the midst of the storm which destroyed many Persian ships off Cape Sepias, the magi offered victims to the winds and charmed them with the help of conjurers, while at the same time they sacrificed to Thetis and the Nereids, to whom they had heard the Sepian promontory was sacred.‡

These are the three religious systems which met in Susa. At this time each had received something from the others, so that their elements were mingled and modified, and neither could stand out entirely separate and distinct. Haman appealed to the lowest form of religious belief—the elemental worship.

---

* Herodotus, vii, 31, 39, 43, 114. † Strabo.
‡ Herodotus, vii, 114, 191.

Among the ancients great attention was paid to lucky and unlucky days. The whole year was divided into lucky and unlucky days, and cuneiform tablets have been recovered on which such days are catalogued. Besides this, special days must be selected for every important enterprise. Haman could not wreak his vengeance on the Jewish nation for a Jewish insult without first having selected a propitious day for the enterprise.

This day might have been selected by appealing to the stars, by inspecting the entrails of sacrificial victims, by watching the flight of birds, by casting lots, and by other means. Haman chose to cast lots.

The lot was not unknown to the Jews. With them it was an appeal to God without bias or passion. The ancients sometimes represent the gods themselves as resorting to divination by the lot. By lot the tribes of Israel were located in Palestine, levitical cities assigned, and after their return from the exile settlements in their homesteads selected. By lot they disposed of prisoners of war and discovered criminals. The sailors cast lots and found Jonah to be the offender to be surrendered to appease the sea. Election to important offices and assignment to official duties were determined by lot. In like manner the scapegoat was selected. The Urim, the Thummim, and the Ephod were used in connection with the lot. The soldiers cast the lot for the possession of the seamless robe of Christ. An apostle was selected by lot to supply the place of Judas. Elections by lot prevailed in the Church as late as the seventh century.

It was in the month Nisan—the former Hebrew name was Abib—according to the Babylonian method of reckoning, the first month of the year, corresponding with the latter part of March and the early part of April. Haman sent for one or more Magian priests, who came into his presence clothed in splendid vestments and bearing the insignia of their priestly functions. First, the days of the month were tried, and the thirteenth was found to be the most propitious; then the months of the year, and the twelfth month, or Adar, was selected. There was an interval of about eleven months before the massacre. It might give the Jews time to prepare to defend themselves, but Haman was a religious man and had appealed to the lot and to the lot he must go. Whatever the danger he must abide by the decision.

His plans having been formed and a propitious day having been selected, he will have little trouble in gaining the consent of the king to issue a royal decree commanding the slaughter.

His proposal to the king is very subtilly calculated. He represents the Jews as dwelling alone, and hence open to suspicion, and as having laws of their own, and hence disloyal to the royal authority. "There is a certain people," said he, "scattered abroad, and dispersed among the people in all the provinces of thy kingdom; and their laws *are* diverse from all people, neither keep they the king's laws: therefore it is not for the king's profit to suffer them." Esther iii, 8.

There was some truth mixed with this falsehood. This, however, rendered the falsehood more dangerous. "So far as regarded religion, it was true that the Jews had laws diverse from all people, neither kept they the king's laws on this head; but this did not interfere with their civil allegiance, and their enemies belied and calumniated them when they insinuated that they did not yield a thankful obedience to the laws of the empire in secular matters." * The same charge has been the apology for many of the great religious persecutions which disgrace the pages of history and the annals of the Church.

"If it please the king, let it be written that they may be destroyed." But the wholesale slaughter of one of the nations of the empire would unfavorably affect the amount of the royal revenues. Hence Haman calls attention to the Oriental custom of confiscating the property of executed criminals, and pledges himself that he will save from the spoils ten thousand talents of silver and pay it over to the king's financiers to be turned into the treasury. This sum of money would equal from ten millions to more than

* McCrie.

twenty millions of dollars, according as we estimate by the civil or by the Mosaic shekel. Haman may have expected to pay this at once from his own private resources and to make all that he could out of the spoils of the massacre. Thus the proposal appealed strongly to the cupidity of both the king and his vizier.

The king, with Oriental courtesy, while appearing to reject, accepts the bribe and gives to Haman his signet-ring to authenticate any document which he wishes to prepare.

The use of the seal belonged to remote antiquity. No document in the East is regarded as authentic unless sealed. In Egypt engraved stones were pierced through lengthwise and hung by a string or chain about the neck or arm, or set in rings to be worn on the finger. An ancient form was the scarabæus, made of stone or blue pottery or porcelain, with an inscription or device on the flat side. The Egyptians, Assyrians, and Babylonians used cylinder-seals of precious stone, or terra-cotta, which they rolled over the document to be sealed. Among the two latter nations the document was frequently of clay, which was sealed while soft and afterward baked or dried. Sometimes the seal consisted of a lump of clay which was impressed with the seal and attached to the document by a string. Doors of tombs were closed and sealed. The importance of sealing is evident from its metaphorical use in the Bible.

SEAL RINGS.

The ring-seal came into use later. "It consisted of a ring, to one side of which a seal was attached, the seal being sometimes stationary, with the inscription upon the outer side only; at other times it was so constructed as to revolve upon its axis, and possessed several inscriptions, which might be used at the option of the wearer. Sometimes the seal was a flat oval disk having inscriptions upon the two opposite surfaces, at other times it was in the form of a cube with inscriptions upon the four sides." *

The custom of using the seal was introduced into Greece and Rome from the East. The importance of the signet-ring illustrates many passages of Scripture.

The seals of Osirtasen I., of Sabaco, and of Cheops, the builder of the Great Pyramid, have been recovered; also the seal which it is thought Pharaoh gave to Joseph, and those of Sennacherib and Darius Hystaspis.

The seal was a symbol of authority, and was parted with only upon extraordinary occasions. It was

* *The Lowell Hebrew Club, The Book of Esther*, p. 141.

used in the place of the sign manual and gave the same validity to documents. When Xerxes gave to Haman his seal he delegated to him supreme authority.

When Cyrus called for volunteers to bring to him Oroetes, dead or alive, thirty of the chief Persians offered themselves for the work. Lots were cast, and Bagaeus was selected to execute the king's wishes. "Then Bagaeus caused many letters to be written on divers matters, and sealed them all with the king's signet; after which he took the letters with him and departed for Sardis. On his arrival he was shown into the presence of Oroetes, when he uncovered the letters one by one, and giving them to the king's secretary—every satrap has with him a king's secretary—commanded him to read their contents. Herein his design was to try the fidelity of the bodyguard, and see if they would be likely to fall away from Oroetes. When, therefore, he saw that they showed the letters all due respect, and even more highly reverenced their contents, he gave the secretary a paper on which was written, 'Persians, King Darius forbids you to guard Oroetes.' The soldiers at these words laid aside their spears. So Bagaeus, finding that they obeyed his mandate, took courage, and gave into the secretary's hands the last letter, wherein it was written, 'King Darius commands the Persians who are in Sardis to kill Oroetes.' Then the guards drew their swords and slew him upon the spot." *

Haman, armed with supreme authority, hastened his preparations. The king's scribes were called, and at Haman's dictation wrote the edict of extermination addressed to the various officers of the provinces and sealed with the king's seal.

"The Jews' enemy" caused the edict to be written in the king's name, thereby rendering it binding and irrevocable. "And the letters were sent by posts into all the king's provinces."

In so mighty an empire rapidity of communication was necessary that the king might be speedily informed concerning the condition of affairs in all its provinces, and that his edicts might be carried as quickly as possible to the utmost limits of the realm. There were then no roads in western Asia; they may scarcely be said to exist at the present day. They are only routes of travel, with no improvements save where they cross the mountains.

In mountainous countries fleet footmen were employed as runners to carry royal dispatches. There is the record of a journey from Tyre to Jerusalem which was accomplished in twenty-four hours. The distance is one hundred miles. Even one hundred and fifty miles have been accomplished in the same time. Saul had an organized body of footmen. Horses,

* Herodotus, iii, 127, 128.

camels, and other swift beasts were employed in the less mountainous regions.

The Persian postal system was established by Cyrus the Great. It was greatly improved by Darius, and afterward by Xerxes.

"Nothing mortal travels so fast as these Persian messengers. The entire plan is a Persian invention; and this is the method of it. Along the whole line of road there are men (they say) stationed, with horses, in number equal to the number of days which the journey takes, allowing a man and horse to each day; and these men will not be hindered from accomplishing at their best speed the distance which they have to go, either by snow or rain, or heat, or by the darkness of night. The first rider delivers his dispatch to the second, and the second passes it to the third; and so it is borne from hand to hand along the whole line, like the light in the torch-race which the Greeks celebrated to Vulcan." *

The post-houses were doubtless still more frequent —at such distances apart that a horse could gallop from one to the next at full speed. Each being provided with several relays of horses and several couriers, the dispatch was forwarded at utmost speed.

Inns were to be found at every station, bridges and fords crossed the streams, and guard-houses with bodies of soldiery protected the messengers from rob-

* Herodotus, viii, 98.

bery or delays from the attacks of brigands. Men could be pressed into the service in cases of necessity, to hasten the dispatches or to protect the king's messengers.

"News of the death of Philotus, and orders for the execution of Parmenio, his father, were carried on dromedaries from near Herat to Ecbatana, a distance of eight hundred and fifty miles, in eleven days." *

This postal system was only for the king's business. The main postal routes in the reign of Xerxes were the route from Susa to Sardis, that from Susa to Babylon, and a branch to Ecbatana. There were less important postal-roads to all parts of the empire.

The materials used for writing in ancient times were various. Public inscriptions and brief records were placed upon stone, metallic, or clay surfaces. Clay cylinders, papyrus rolls, waxed tablets, and parchment were often used for books. Parchment was employed in western Asia for all missive documents. Sometimes preparations were made from box-wood, palm-leaves, and linen.

Besides the cuneiform character adapted to the chisel, there probably existed in Persia an alphabet better adapted to the pen. "The pen was usually of reed, with a metallic pointed style for wax, and still harder tools for stone or plaster or metal; and the prevalent ink was a mixture of gall and lampblack."

* Strabo, xv, ii, 10.

The following copy of an ancient letter will be interesting: "Areus, king of the Lacedæmonians, to Onias, sendeth greeting. We have met with a certain writing whereby we have discovered that both the Jews and Lacedæmonians are of one stock, and are derived from the kindred of Abraham. It is but just, therefore, that you, who are our brethren, should send to us about any of your concerns as you please. We will also do the same thing, and esteem your concerns as our own, and will look upon our concerns as in common with yours. Demoteles, who brings you this letter, will bring your answer back to us." This letter is foursquare; and the seal is an eagle, with a dragon in its claws.*

The king's scribes soon completed copies of the bloody edict in all the languages of the principal nations of the kingdom—"to destroy, to kill, and to cause to perish, all Jews, both young and old, little children and women, in one day, *even* upon the thirteenth *day* of the twelfth month, which *is* the month Adar, and *to take* the spoil of them for a prey." The scribe certified the writing in the words: "The copy of the writing, for a commandment to be given in every province, was published unto all people, that they should be ready against that day."

It was entirely consistent with the custom of the Persians and other ancient nations to put to death

* *The Lowell Hebrew Club, The Book of Esther*, pp. 121, 122.

not only the criminal himself, but also his wife and children.*

The couriers received the edict, published it in Susa, and sped in every direction into all the provinces of the empire " pressed on by the command of the king."

Why this so great haste in publishing the edict when it would be eleven months before the day selected by lot for the slaughter? The Jews would take warning and flee from the kingdom. What cared Haman? He would be well rid of the hated race, and he could see to it that they carried little of their property with them in their flight.

But the people of "Shushan the palace" and of Susa, the city, were alarmed. The great majority of them were doubtless friendly to the Jews. And then, too, they feared for their own safety. If Xerxes has ordered the massacre of the Jewish nation this year, what nation will be exterminated next year?

"And the king and Haman sat down to drink; but the city Shushan was perplexed."

* Herodotus, iii, 119.

CHAPTER XI.

SUSPENSE, AGONY, RESOLUTION.

"Mordecai rent his clothes."—ESTHER iv, 1.

"*There was* great mourning among the Jews, and fasting, and weeping and wailing."—ESTHER iv, 3.

"Who knoweth whether thou art come to the kingdom for *such* a time as this?"—ESTHER iv, 14.

"Fast ye for me, and neither eat nor drink three days, night or day: . . . if I perish, I perish."—ESTHER iv, 16.

THE decree of the king will be executed. The annihilation of the Jewish nation is certain. Monarchs of even later times have shown themselves equal to any atrocity. Tamerlane, in his march against Delhi, massacred one hundred thousand captives, and having stormed Bagdad, piled ninety thousand corpses in public places as a terror to his enemies. He put to death all the inhabitants of Ispahan, except her artists and scholars. Seventy thousand heads were piled up in the form of towers. At Sebsewar two thousand persons were piled up alive, their heads outward and their bodies built up with mortar. The Janizaries in Constantinople were butchered to the number of twenty-five thousand. This was in 1826. In 1821 the Turks, by slaughter and enslavement, destroyed more than one hundred thousand of the

Christian population of Scio. The Koords butchered ten thousand of the Nestorians in 1843. It was but in the year 1861 that the Turks and Druses slaughtered the Christians of Mt. Lebanon—"eleven thousand Christians massacred; one hundred thousand sufferers by the civil war; twenty thousand desolate widows and orphans; three thousand Christian habitations burned; and property to the value of ten millions of dollars (gold) destroyed." Not only is the edict of Xerxes itself credible, but it is also certain that such an edict would have been executed.

No wonder that "when Mordecai perceived all that was done, Mordecai rent his clothes, and put on sackcloth with ashes, and went out *into the* midst of the city, and cried *with a* loud and a bitter cry." If was not because of his fear of personal harm. If the royal edict had devoted himself alone to death, he could have received it with the silence, the equanimity, and the courage of a Daniel. Nor was it because of the doom which hung over his royal relative, the beautiful queen. That, even, would not have called forth such violent expressions of grief. But the whole Jewish nation was doomed. And another consideration which caused this to weigh more heavily was the fact that he himself was instrumental in bringing this calamity upon his people. Not that he repented because of what he had done. He had counted the cost of disobedience, and would stand his ground. But it must have been a most painful reflection for him to know that he had been the occasion of this explosion of the Satanic rage of the Jews' enemy.

The expression of his grief was in the true Oriental spirit. He rent his clothes, put on sackcloth, sprinkled ashes upon his person, went out into the streets of the city, and cried with a loud and bitter cry. This was Jewish; it was also Persian, and Oriental.

"At Susa, on the arrival of the first message, which said that Xerxes was master of Athens, such was the delight of the Persians who had remained behind, that they forthwith strewed all the streets with myrtle boughs, and burnt incense, and fell to feasting and merriment. In like manner, when the second message reached them, so sore was their dismay that they all with one accord rent their garments, and cried aloud, and wept and wailed without stint." *

"When the horse reached the camp, Mardonius and all the Persian army made great lamentation for Masistius. They shaved off all the hair from their own heads, and cut the manes from their war-horses and their sumpter-beasts, while they vented their grief in such loud cries that all Bœotia resounded with the clamor, because they had lost the man who, next to Mardonius, was held in the greatest esteem, both by the king and by the Persians generally." †

* Herodotus, viii, 99. † *Ibid.*, ix, 24.

When the Persians saw Cambyses at the approach of death bewail his misfortunes, they "rent the garments that they had on, and uttered lamentable cries." * Æschylus in "The Persians" does not exaggerate this grief and its expression. † The Egyptians were equally violent in expressions of mourning. ‡

Esau, like Mordecai, "cried with a great and exceeding bitter cry." Gen. xxvii, 34. Daniel sought the Lord, clothed in sackcloth and covered with ashes. Dan. ix, 3. All the scriptural modes of expressing grief and mourning are to be found in Job ii, 12, and elsewhere.

Thus Mordecai went forth into the streets of the city, in the intense anguish of his soul, and his piercing cries ceased not to weary the very heavens. The loud wailing called many from their dwellings, and they beheld the object of pity, clothed with a coarse cloth of hair and covered with ashes, passing slowly along the streets, smiting upon his breast or raising his hands to heaven and ever giving utterance to the same piercing cries. As the news of the bloody decree spread, the Jews everywhere joined in the wail of grief, and clothed themselves in the garb of mourning. And with the speed of the king's mes-

* Herodotus, iii, 66. Comp. iii, 64; vii, 45.
† Æschylus, *The Persians*, 251-285; 570-585; 702-1045.
‡ Herodotus, ii, 85.

sengers it extended throughout the provinces of the empire. Ashes were sprinkled upon the ground to become the bed of those whose grief was intense.

"There was great mourning among the Jews, and fasting, and weeping, and wailing: and many lay in sackcloth and ashes."*

Mordecai, in his aimless wandering or with some undefined purpose, approaches the king's gate, but is arrested by the guard, "for none might enter into the king's gate clothed with sackcloth."

"It was contrary to every established rule, and an offense highly punishable, for any one to appear within the precincts of the palace of the Persian kings in the dress or with the look of a mourner. There must be nothing seen there to remind the sovereign that trouble and suffering are experienced by mortals. With every luxury to gratify his pampered appetite, with external splendor to please his eye, and sweet music to soothe his ear, and the flattery of courtiers to make him regard himself as something more than mortal, he passed his life in seclusion from all sights and sounds of distress and woe." †

"But thus to keep out the badges of sorrow, unless they could withal have kept out the causes of sorrow, to forbid sackcloth to enter, unless they could have forbidden sickness and trouble and death to enter, was jest." ‡

* Comp. Isaiah lviii, 5; Jonah iii, 6. † Davidson. ‡ Henry.

The only words joyful to the ear of the monarch would have been, "Let the king live forever." There are scriptural references to this law of the palace. Gen. 1, 4; Neh. ii, 1. How little the king knows of the sorrow of his subject! how little the rich know of the troubles of the poor!

The servants of Esther seem to have learned her relation to Mordecai, though they were not yet informed of his nationality. They had observed his profound grief, and reported it to the queen. His royal cousin fell into convulsive anguish at the sad news brought by her servants, but recovering, in a measure, her composure, sent garments to induce him to lay aside his sackcloth, enter the king's gate, and relate to her the cause of his poignant grief. But what was her surprise when she was told that Mordecai failed to comply with a request which, coming from the queen, should have been his law! The circumstances must have been most extraordinary which would have justified such a course. Some awful calamity must be impending.

Esther sends for her most trusted servant, Hatach, and commissions him to go to Mordecai and learn the nature of the trouble. Hatach finds him in the street in front of the gate of the palace. Mordecai reveals to him the whole history—the offense, the sum of money which Haman promised to pay into the treasury as the price of blood, the edict of slanghter, the day selected for its execution, and its publication throughout all the provinces of the empire by the king's messengers. He gives him also a copy of the decree, that the queen may know the full enormity of its wickedness. In conclusion, he charges him to enjoin upon the queen the duty of going to the king and supplicating him to spare her people.

This is a dangerous mission. She must reveal herself as one of the people who have been condemned to death. She must oppose Haman, the king's most powerful favorite. She must ask him to do something that is impossible—change a law of the Medes and Persians.

More obvious objections to the course proposed come to her mind. She has reason to doubt whether she is any longer the king's favorite. His affections seem to have been transferred to another. At least she has not been called to come to the king's apartments for thirty days.* He would, doubtless, not be in a proper temper to listen to her petition, much less to give a favorable response. An obstacle more formidable still presented itself. "All the king's servants and the people of the king's provinces *do* know that whosoever, *whether* man or woman, shall come unto the king *into* the inner court, who is not called, *there is* one law of his to put *him* to death, except *such* to whom the king shall hold out the

* Herodotus, iii, 69.

golden scepter, that he may live." She cannot hope that the king will hold out the golden scepter to her, especially if he has transferred his affections to a more favored wife.

When Hatach presents the urgent request of Mordecai to Esther, she can only command his return to her cousin to inform him of obstacles in the way which seem to her to be absolutely insurmountable—her want of influence with the king, and the difficulty of access to his presence.

Among the resolutions adopted by the seven conspirators who placed Darius upon the throne of Persia was this: "It was to be free to each, whenever he pleased, to enter the palace unannounced, unless the king were in the company of one of his wives."

"Of the seven Persians who rose up against the Magus, one, Intaphernes, lost his life very shortly after the outbreak for an act of insolence. He wished to enter the palace and transact a certain business with the king. Now the law was that all those who had taken part in the rising against the Magus might enter unannounced into the king's presence, unless he happened to be in private with his wife. So Intaphernes would not have any one announce him, but, as he belonged to the seven, claimed it as his right to go in. The door-keeper, however, and chief usher forbade his entrance, since the king, they said, was with his wife. But Intaphernes thought they told lies; so, drawing his scymitar, he cut off their noses and their ears, and, hanging them on the bridle of his horse, put the bridle round their necks, and so let them go."

Intaphernes, with all his family and all his relatives, save his wife and her brother and eldest son, was slain.*

Great ceremony was required in all that pertained to the court. When a person was ushered into the royal presence, he must not step on the royal carpet, he must keep his hands concealed in his sleeves, and he must prostrate himself before the king. It was a capital crime to sit on the royal throne, and a high offense to wear the clothing which the king had cast off.

"Etiquette was almost as severe on the monarch himself as on his subjects. He was required to live chiefly in seclusion; to eat his meals, for the most part, alone; never to go on foot beyond the palace walls; never to revoke an order once given, however much he might regret it; never to draw back from a promise, whatever ill results he might anticipate from its performance. To maintain the quasi-divine character attached to him it was necessary that he should seem infallible, immutable, and wholly free from the weakness of repentance." †

---

* Herodotus, iii, 84, 118, 119; comp. Josephus, *Antiquities*, xi, 6, 3.
† Rawlinson.

The scepter may have been originally a simple staff on which to lean, or a shepherd's crook. Among nations to whom the agricultural life was the earliest known we do not find the symbolic shepherd's staff. According to Diodorus Siculus the scepter of the Egyptian kings bore the shape of a plow. Saul carried his javelin as a symbol of power. On the monuments the king is always represented with scepter in hand. To lean the scepter toward a person was the sign of royal favor; and to kiss or touch its top was the sign of submission.

When Hatach presents the message from the queen, reciting to Mordecai the difficulties and dangers in the way of obedience to his request, he finds him determined, and ready with new arguments. Mordecai looks to the palace for sympathy, and knows that there is an intercessor at court. God's providence may be active in behalf of the Jews, but it needs Mordecai's faith, and Esther's courage.

First of all, Mordecai reminds her of her own personal peril. Her high position will be no protection. Her nationality will certainly become known, and there would be found more than one in the king's palace who, from hate or envy or jealousy, would delight to strike so shining a mark. And then again, God will certainly save a remnant of his people. "*Then* shall *there* enlargement and deliverance arise to the Jews." Other instruments will be found if they fail, but for her disobedience to the divine call she shall not escape. These were stout words to speak to a Persian queen, but the necessity was imperative. The Jews who perform their duty will not be destroyed. "We have this noble and clearly heroic faith of Mordecai, which sees the future deliverance, even amid the most immediate and imminent danger."* Only the recreant will suffer.

The all-convincing argument was still to be given. Esther's history had been remarkable—an orphan in exile, by a wonderful train of providential circumstances raised to the throne of the mightiest empire in the world. It is not without design that God has so ordered. It must have been to meet some great emergency. The emergency has come. "Who knoweth whether thou art come to the kingdom for *such a* time as this?"

"The suggestion of Providence being concerned in the matter was like life from the dead to Esther. The idea of Providence having been now some time working up to this point was an immense comfort and impulse to her mind. It was a flash of light that lit up the whole scene for a moment. And when that one moment was sped, the darkness that returned was not, as before, unrelieved. There was a distinct line of light athwart it. Confidence as to

* Brenz.

the final issue of all was far from present. Nothing like absolute conviction that in the end all would be well could Esther boast. Suspense in some shape still prolonged its unwelcome sojourn. But it was no longer the agonized suspense of not knowing what to do, of not knowing whether to move at all. The pent-up heart is bad enough, but solitary confinement must make it much worse. Pent-up hope is a terrible strain, but the strain becomes much worse when it must be tolerated without one active effort, one healthy struggle. This phase of things had now passed by for Esther. She had gone faithfully through it, and was none the worse for having treated it as a thing that needed to be gone through faithfully and unhurriedly. Mordecai was not necessarily in the right when he seemed to wonder at Esther's hesitation. Though we credit him with being a wise man, a good man, and very full of pride in Esther and love to her, Esther very likely felt that he had not put himself quite in her position, and could not do so. But it was because she had gone faithfully through the struggle, and well looked at the question on both sides, and considered its alternative difficulties and perils, that when enough light did come she used it in a moment; and when thought had done its fair amount of work, hesitation fled, and determination succeeded to its place. To wearied human inquiry, to exhausted human resources, to bewildered human wisdom, comes in most welcome the ministry, little thought of before, of the Invisible."

Esther had decided to go into the presence of the king, and thus break a royal law, and to make a request which it was impossible for the king to grant, and which at the same time would reveal her nationality, and her hostility to the most powerful royal favorite, and oppose the king's edict, while it would declare herself and all her relatives condemned to death as criminals and traitors by an irreversible sentence. But she would not venture her life upon this perilous mission without special religious preparation, and the assistance of the prayers of God's chosen people.

So great is the influence which she has gained over her maids and the other servants of her palace that she knows that she can depend upon their sympathy, and that they will join with her in a strict fast, which shall have no interruption till the third day. They will spend the time in humiliation, repentance, and supplication before God. She commands Mordecai to assemble the Jews of Shushan, and with them observe a religious fast during the same time.

The beautiful queen and her maids are in earnest, tearful supplication, Mordecai and the Jews are crying before God, and the city Shushan is perplexed; but Xerxes and Haman sit and drink their wine.

The Fast of Esther is observed annually on the thirteenth of the month Adar, to commemorate that dark day. This fast gave way, during the Maccabæan period and for some years later, to a festival celebrating the victory of the Jews under Judas Maccabæus over Nicanor. This festival ceased to be celebrated, and in the ninth century the Fast of Esther was again instituted and has been celebrated annually since that date. On this day there is neither eating nor drinking, but penitential songs are sung and special prayers offered. When the thirteenth of Adar comes on the Sabbath the fast is observed on Friday. Some Jews, following the example of Esther, fast three days.

How this fast was observed by the Jews of Shushan may be learned by reference to Jewish customs as revealed in the Scriptures. 1 Kings xxi, 27-29; Neh. i, 4; Joel i, 14; Jonah iii, 5 *et. seq.*

Esther was strengthened in her purpose. Her faith was brighter. She recognized the hand of Providence. She saw her supreme opportunity. She became a magnificent heroine. The conflict of emotions had ceased. Self had unconditionally capitulated. She resolved and— "if I perish, I perish." These are not the words of despair, not the words of stoicism, not the words of one so exhausted as to become indifferent; they are the words of heroic resignation. Gen. xliii, 14.

The real victory of Esther was the victory of faith.

The hand of Haman had set in motion fearful machinery. The engine of destruction was advancing and would overtake and crush all. Mordecai, with undefined faith and uncertain hope, kept near the palace, as if to remain close as possible to one who must have sadly needed his sympathy, advice, and prayers. He could do nothing more. Esther must, at the last, bear the awful responsibility alone. While on the one hand she was moved by the tenderest considerations, in her love for Mordecai and her loyalty to her own people, on the other hand there were tormenting apprehensions in regard to the issue of the course proposed. Interests of incalculable moment depended upon her decision. Lives and hearts and things most sacred were in her hands—if God but prospered her appeals. How much depended upon one woman! How valuable appeared then a single life! She was compelled to contend with the most aggravating contradictions. On the one side, love of kindred, duty to God, the expostulations of Mordecai, his command, the momentum of long obedience, fear of personal harm, patriotism, and religion, impelled her to go to the king; on the other side, possible disgrace and death, with the failure of the whole effort and the occasion for hastening and rendering more thorough the slaughter of her people. What should Esther do? Never was poor mortal compelled to decide a more difficult question. The ruling appeal at the last was the religious. "A woman's discernment is notably quick, and her sight intuition, and the eye of Esther opened and met the eye of Heaven falling on her and on all her anxiety." This resolve, this victory of faith, this supreme capitulation of self, made her one of the greatest heroines of sacred history.

XII.

MAGNIFICENT HEROISM, MASTERLY DELAY, WAKEFUL PROVIDENCE.

"The king held out to Esther the golden scepter."—ESTHER v, 2.
"What *is* thy petition? and it shall be granted thee."—ESTHER v, 6.
"Let the king and Haman come to the banquet."—ESTHER v, 8.
"Then went Haman forth that day joyful and with a glad heart."—ESTHER v, 9.
"All this availeth me nothing."—ESTHER v, 13.
"Let a gallows be made."—ESTHER v, 14.

At the close of the fast, "on the third day," Esther prepared to petition the king. She neglected no precaution that might increase the probabilities of success. She put on her "royal apparel"—the love tokens of her husband—to awaken again his early affections.

"The hour was one which found incalculable human interests at stake. The blotting out of existence, the swift swallowing up of human lives innumerable, with all their precious freightage of love and joy, of purpose and hope, was no light fancy, no vague fear now. Yet that was the appalling uncertainty beneath the burden of which the solemn hour bended. It was not dull cloudiness of sky alone, and that made worse by unnecessary apprehension and weak fearfulness. It was one defined dark mass of cloud. To all human appearance the question of the hour depended on the caprice of one man. It did not resemble some case of great interest, which was going

KING ON HIS THRONE.

to have the best attention of a select number of the best of people, and thereupon a deliberate decision be taken. In that hour the *momentary whim* of a capricious despot would decide the question of life or death, for the innocent Esther first, and after her for a whole race, of which she was then the head and representative." *

She "stood in the inner court of the king's house, over against the king's house: and the king sat upon his royal throne in the royal house, over against the gate of the house." Esther v, 1.

"There she stands, with her jeweled foot upon the grave. A noble spectacle! not so much for her unrivaled beauty, still less for the splendor of her apparel, as for the resolution to venture life, and either save her nation or perish in the attempt. In her blooming youth, in the admiration of the court, in the affection of her husband, in her lofty rank, in her queenly honor, she has every thing to make life attractive. Hers is a golden cup, and it is foaming with pleasure to the brim. But her mind is made up to die, and so with a silent prayer, and 'If I perish, I perish' on her lips, she passes in, and now stands mute and pallid, yet calm and resolute, outside the ring of nobles to hear her doom. Nor has she to endure the agony of a long suspense. Her fate, which seems to tremble in the balance, is soon determined. No sooner does the monarch catch sight of the beautiful woman, and brave and good as beautiful, whom he had raised from slavery to share his bed and throne, than her apprehensions vanish; the clouds

* Barker.

break, and she finds, as we often do with Christ, that her fears had wronged her lord. Presently his hand stretches out the golden scepter; the business of the court is stopped. 'The queen! the queen!' divides the crowd of nobles; and up that brilliant lane she walks in majesty and in charms that outvie her gems, to hear the blessed words, 'What wilt thou, Queen Esther? and what is thy request? it shall be even given thee to the half of the kingdom.'" *

The sight of a speaking human face is ever the strongest argument to secure love, sympathy, trust, and help. Personal presence is a powerful indorsement to a petition.

There were many reasons why Esther should not at that time present her petition. She was not sure of the king. She must not interpret too literally his extravagant Oriental promise. Such promises were not uncommon, and were fulfilled when the heart of the king was right.

Herod swore to the daughter of Herodias, "Whatsoever thou shalt ask of me, I will give it thee, unto the half of my kingdom." Mark vi, 23.

At Sardis Xerxes contracted a passion for the wife of Masistes. His advances were not encouraged by the noble woman, and he had great respect for and fear of Masistes, who was his brother. To accomplish his ends he betrothed his own son Darius to the

* Guthrie.

daughter of Masistes, but upon receiving the newly married couple in his palace at Susa he lost his old love and conceived a passion for Artaÿnta, the wife of Masistes' son.

"Amestris, the wife of Xerxes, had woven with her own hands a long robe of many colors, and very curious, which she presented to her husband as a gift. Xerxes, who was greatly pleased with it, forthwith put it on, and went in to visit Artaÿnta, who happened likewise on this day to please him greatly. He therefore bade her ask him whatever boon she liked, and promised that, whatever it was, he would assuredly grant her request. Then Artaÿnta, who was doomed to suffer calamity with all her house, said to him, 'Wilt thou indeed give me whatever I like to ask?' So the king, suspecting nothing less than that her choice would fall where it did, pledged his word, and swore to her. She then, as soon as she heard his oath, asked boldly for the robe. Hereupon Xerxes tried all possible means to avoid the gift, not that he grudged to give it, but because he dreaded Amestris, who already suspected, and would now, he feared, detect his love. So he offered her cities instead, and heaps of gold, and an army which should obey no other leader. (The last of these is a thoroughly Persian gift.) But, as nothing could prevail on Artaÿnta to change her mind, at the last he gave her the robe. Then Artaÿnta was very greatly rejoiced, and she often wore the garment and was proud of it. And so it came to the ears of Amestris that the robe had been given to her."

On the king's birthday he gave a great royal banquet, as was the custom. The law of such a feast was that no one who asked a boon, whatever it might be, should be denied his request. When, therefore, Amestris asked for the wife of Masistes, whom she justly blamed for the love which Xerxes bore to Artaÿnta, he could not refuse the boon. "At length, however, wearied by her importunity, and constrained moreover by the law of the feast, which required that no one who asked a boon that day at the king's board should be denied his request, he yielded, but with a very ill will, and gave the wife of Masistes into her power." Xerxes now endeavored in vain to persuade Masistes to put away his wife, even promising him his own daughter in marriage.

"While these things were passing between Xerxes and his brother Masistes, Amestris sent for the spearmen of the royal body-guard, and caused the wife of Masistes to be mutilated in a horrible fashion. Her two breasts, her nose, ears, and lips were cut off and thrown to the dogs; her tongue was torn out by the roots, and thus disfigured she was sent back to her home." Masistes now hastened to Bactria, over which he was satrap, intending to avenge himself by stirring up a revolt among the Bactrians and Sacans, but

Xerxes, learning his designs, sent an army which overtook him and slew him and his sons and all his followers. "Such is the tale of king Xerxes' love and of the death of his brother Masistes."* But Esther was to make a larger request than these, and must be sure of her ground.

Again, it would not be wise to present her petition in the presence of the court. Haman was the Prime Minister, and had doubtless made many influential friends, who would save him if his life were threatened. If the queen could gain a private audience with the king, and have Haman present, she could then accuse him to his face. Such a course of delay would be in strict accordance with Oriental usage. "In presenting a request to a superior, it is extremely common to begin with an outlying, subordinate matter, and have the answer, the argument, or the battle over that. If the petition is received favorably, it will be easy to ask a little more, and so on up to the thing really desired. Thus the entire matter is not compromised, nor either the petitioner or the petitioned committed finally by the first refusal. Of course the one petitioned often sees through the whole from the start; but on the one hand it is a form, and on the other hand it is a useful form—two good reasons for keeping it up. Sometimes the petitioned cuts short the petitioner at the start, and goes on

* Herodotus, ix, 108–113.

from his own intuition to grant the whole desired favor."* Solomon had the grace to refuse the final request after the general promise. 1 Kings ii, 13–25. Xerxes may do the same.

The only safety is for the queen to delay. So she invites the king and Haman on that day to a banquet which she has prepared. The king usually dines alone, or with the queen or queen-mother, or with his children or one or two brothers. It is an extraordinary favor to invite a guest who is not a member of the royal family. Haman may well consider himself highly honored. The king graciously accepts the invitation, and commands notice to be given at once to Haman, who does not seem to be present, that he may hasten his preparations and be at the banquet in due season.

The king and Haman went to the banquet, and we may be sure that Esther neglected nothing that might give pleasure to her royal husband. The banquet was terminated by a special banquet of wine, at which they sat long; drinking the wine of Helbon and eating a great variety of highly seasoned delecacies. It was doubtless when the king's heart was "merry" that he repeated his question, "What *is* thy petition? and it shall be granted thee."

Esther began to answer, "My petition and my request"—but her heart failed her. She saw, as by an

* Isaac H. Hall.

instantaneous flash of wisdom, that her best hope was in further delay. So she ended by inviting them to a similar banquet which she would prepare for the next day. The inspiration which brought her to this decision was most happy, as we shall see, for events ripened rapidly which led to the climax of the tragedy.

Haman went out from the banquet "joyful and with a glad heart." He had reached the height of his ambition. He was next to the king. People bowed before him as they did before the monarch himself. His word was law. He, of all the great men of his time, enjoyed the confidence of the queen and was honored by her equally with the king. But in passing the king's gate he saw Mordecai the Jew— who bowed not, neither trembled in his presence. Dignified and self-possessed, he did not notice great Haman. The latter was "full of indignation," but with an effort refrained himself. He might have ordered an attendant to thrust him through with the sword, and it would have been done; but he meditated a sweeter vengeance.

After having had ample leisure to reflect upon his conduct in refusing homage to Haman, Mordecai was only confirmed in his course.

"There's a picture! standing out in bold relief, and contrasted with that of the proud but worthless premier. The one haughty and enraged; the other humble, but composed and dignified. It is not the port, the state, the pageantry; it is not the rank, the riches, or power; the mind and spirit—*that* is the man. The person who occupies the place of a common porter may have within him a soul that towers in real greatness far above that of the proudest and most titled grandee. He may have that within him which, while it rouses the indignation, quails the courage of him who has armies at his back. He who is conscious of acting rightly has no reason to grow pale at the sight of danger. He who is embarked in the cause of God and his people, and whose conscience acquits him of having failed in his duty to his prince, or of having done evil to any man, feels himself clad in the panoply of heaven; stands fearless and scathless, is immovable in his purpose, and will not do a mean or unworthy, far less a sinful thing, to save his own life, or the lives of those whom he holds dearest." *

Reaching home, Haman sends for his friends and flatterers, and when they have gathered, and his wife also is present, he parades before them his fortune and honors. He has amassed great wealth. Evidently he had made his position serve his selfishness and covetousness. His magnificent offer of ten thousand talents for the property of the Jews was doubtless in keeping with his shrewd business and avaricious instincts. His second boast was his mul-

* M'Crie.

titude of children — being ten sons. "Next to prowess in arms, it is regarded as the grandest proof of manly excellence to be the father of many sons. Every year the king sends rich gifts to the man who can show the largest number: for they hold that number is strength."*

"Sheikh Ali Mirza, a son of the well-known Futteh Ali Shah, was accounted the proudest and happiest man in the empire, because, when he rode out on state occasions, he was attended by a body-guard of sixty of his own sons. At the time of Futteh Ali Shah's death his direct decendants amounted to nearly three thousand, some of them being in the fifth degree, and every Persian in consequence felt a pride in being the subject of such a king. The greatest misfortune, indeed, that can befall a man in Persia is to be childless. When a chief's '*hearthstone*,' as it was said, '*was dark*,' he lost all respect, and hence arose the now universal practice of adoption."†

"The kings propose annual prizes for a numerous family of children."‡ It was a great blessing, among orientals, to possess a large family of sons.

Again, the king had promoted Haman to the highest office in the kingdom, save only the throne itself. This was pleasing not only because of its proof of kingly favor, its honors, and its emoluments, but more

---

* Herodotus, i, 136.   † H. C. Rawlinson.   ‡ Strabo, xv, 3, 17.

especially because "he had advanced him above the princes and servants of the king." He could look *down* upon all these.

Finally, he concludes: "Yea, Esther the queen did let no man come in with the king unto the banquet that she had prepared but myself; and to morrow am I invited unto her also with the king." Esther v, 12.

No man has ever found happiness in such worldly gifts. The human heart wants something more—*something different.* The material universe cannot fill one single soul. Haman confesses that all his honors and all his riches give him "no satisfaction." There is one drop of gall in his cup—Mordecai sits at the king's gate. To be sure, he will soon be slain with all his hated race. But how can Haman wait?

Haman enjoyed the confidence of his own family. He could rely upon their loyalty. He knew that within his own home and within the circle of his friends he could find sympathy. He opened to them all his heart.

Zeresh, his wife, is equal to the emergency. She will remove the difficulty. Like Jezebel, she proposes heroic treatment. All his friends second her plan. In her indignation and rage against the Jew she speaks impulsively and to the point. "Let a gallows be made of fifty cubits high, and to-morrow speak thou unto the king that Mordecai may be hanged thereon: then go thou in merrily with the king unto the banquet." *There* is the solution to the problem. No one will dare thereafter to neglect to pay proper homage to great Haman.

The plan commends itself to the judgment of Haman. It is speedy, effective, and final. Why had he not thought of that before? The carpenters are employed and immediately set to work. The "gallows" is erected.

The king will grant the reasonable request for permission to put Mordecai to death. We have seen how he gave the life of the wife of Masistes to Amestris. He cannot deny Haman.

CHAPTER XIII.

WHEELS WITHIN WHEELS.

"On that night could not the king sleep."—ESTHER vi, 1.

"What shall be done unto the man whom the king delighteth to honor?"—ESTHER vi, 6.

"Do even so to Mordecai."—ESTHER vi, 10.

The king of this vast empire of kingdoms was powerless to command his own sleep. That very night this fickle servant escaped and fled from him, and, pursue as he might, he could not overtake and secure the fugitive. To beguile his weary hours, as he tossed upon his restless couch, a secretary was commanded to bring the record of the daily affairs and to read to him therefrom.* While reading from this official document, the secretary came to that part of the chronicles in which it was related that Mordecai discovered the conspiracy of Bigthana and Teresh, and saved the king's life. The king became interested in the history, and at the close of the account inquires, "What honor and dignity hath been done to Mordecai for this?" He learns that the service has received no recognition beyond the mere record of the fact.

* Esther ii, 23; Ezra iv, 15, 19; Herodotus, vii, 100; viii, 90; Tacitus, Annals xiii, 31.

From a sense of gratitude, and to more perfectly secure his own personal future safety, the king could not permit such a service to remain unrewarded. Indeed his conscience condemned him for neglecting so imperative an obligation so long. He will attend to the matter as speedily as possible.

In Persia the king's benefactors were adequately rewarded. Their names were placed on a special roll. Themistocles the Athenian received magnificent recognition from the great king. "The king assigned to him, for bread, Magnesia, which produced a revenue of fifty talents in the year; for wine, Lampsacus, which was considered to be the richest in wine of any district then known; and Myus for meat."* Xerxes rewarded with rich gifts those of his satraps who brought their troops to Sardis in the most gallant array when the great army gathered for the invasion of Greece.† Darius gave the Democêdes who was to act as guide to the fifteen Persians who were sent to explore the sea-coast of Greece, "a merchantship laden with all manner of precious things," for presents to his father and brothers.‡

Cyrus the younger, wishing to honor Syennesis, king of Cilicia, presented him with "a horse with a golden bit, a golden chain and golden bracelets, and a golden scimetar and a Persian robe." He promised to each of the Greeks who accompanied him on his

---

*Thucydides, i, 138.   †Herodotus, vii, 26.   ‡*Ibid.*, iii, 135.

expedition, besides other rewards, "a golden crown." The retreating Greeks gave him who had guided them to the sea " a horse, a silver cup, a Persian robe, and ten darics." *

Xerxes on his march to Greece honored the Acanthians by the gift of a Median robe. The conspirators who slew Pseudo-Smerdis, and placed Darius Hystaspis upon the throne of Persia, gave Otanes, one of their number who withdrew from the candidacy, as a special honor, a Median robe each year. Artaxerxes presented to Mithridates, who gave Cyrus his first wound, " a robe embroidered with gold, bracelets and a chain, and a scimetar." †

The three young men of the king's body guard expected to receive from Darius, as a gift to him who showed the highest wisdom, " great gifts, and great tokens of victory; as, to be clothed in purple, and to drink in gold, and to sleep upon gold, and a chariot with gold-studded bridles, and a tiara of byssus, and a chain about his neck; and he shall sit next to Darius because of his wisdom and be called Darius' kinsman." Esdras iii, 6, 7. Joseph gave his brethren changes of raiment. Gen. xl, 22. When the king of Syria sent to the king of Israel Naaman to be recovered of his leprosy, he accompanied his request

---

* Xenophon, Anabasis I, ii, 27; I, vii, 5; IV, vii, 27.

† Herodotus, vii, 116; iii, 83, 84, Xenophon, Anabasis I, ix, 22–26, Plutarch, vol. iii, p. 447.

with a present of "ten talents of silver, and six thousand pieces of gold, and ten changes of raiment." 2 Kings v, 5. Among the presents which "the kings of the earth" brought to Solomon was "raiment." 2 Chron. ix, 24.

Royalty's benefactors sometimes waited long for their reward. In some cases they were doubtless entirely forgotten.*

The king's sleepless night was great with issues which were destined to affect the whole empire, and the religious history of the Jews and THE WORLD. Providence was also sleepless. The deeds of a good man were not forgotten. Mordecai must receive a kingly reward. The chosen people of God were not forgotten.

Haman was stirring early in the morning. The gallows had been finished. He hastened to the royal palace to receive orders for the execution of Mordecai. On that day he wished to go to the queen's banquet "merrily," with nothing to mar his perfect satisfaction and his perfect happiness. He was now waiting in the court for the announcement to be made that the king was ready for the transaction of business. It would not be many minutes thereafter before Mordecai would be impaled upon a stake so high as to be seen by the whole population of Susa. Then the joy of the king's favorite would be full.

* Herodotus, v, 11; iii, 138, 140.

No one would dare, after this example of vengeance, to withhold his homage.

By some movement on the part of the guard the king learns that some one is in the court, and inquires who it is. He is informed that it is Haman, and bids him enter.

"So Haman came in. And the king said unto him, What shall be done unto the man whom the king delighteth to honor?"

And now we meet with a rare exhibition of supreme selfishness. The king could be thinking of no one but Haman. It was not possible that there lived a man whom he could delight to honor more than his all-powerful favorite, before whom the people bowed and who alone of all the great men of the empire had been twice invited by the queen to share with her and the king a specially prepared banquet. So thought Haman.

"It was not only self, but self in the shape of insufferable vanity. It mounted to the pitch of morbid vanity. Some are hurried on by selfishness headlong. But it is a sleek, a smiling, a self-garlanded victim we have here. To the dignity of position already belonging to him fuller gratification (as has been seen) is offered; but it is not *honor* that his eye can see, that his mind can appreciate. The grace and the force of his honored position weigh nothing with him. But the most egotistic *vanity* shuts out, and at a most critical moment, the very idea of the barest possibility of a worthy competitor with himself! He cannot credit the notion of a fellow-creature to compare with himself." *

Having quickly decided who the person must be whom the king delighted to honor, Haman looked about for some appropriate recognition of his extraordinary virtues. He had a most difficult task. He had already received the highest honors in the gift of both the king and the queen. Nothing higher could be conceived, except to be raised to the throne itself. But Haman had a fertile mind, and was equal to the emergency. He could for a time assume the insignia of royalty and receive the homage due only to the king.

So Haman answered: "Let the royal apparel be brought which the king *useth* to wear, and the horse that the king rideth upon, and the crown royal which is set upon his head; and let this apparel and horse be delivered to the hand of one of the king's most noble princes, that they may array the man *withal* whom the king delighteth to honor, and bring him on horseback through the street of the city, and proclaim before him, Thus shall it be done to the man whom the king delighteth to honor." Esther vi, 9.

This was a higher honour than that which the Pharaoh bestowed upon Joseph. Gen. lxi, 42, 43.

* Barker.

To wear a dress which had been previously worn by the king was a capital offense, yet it might be allowed.*

Arrian tells the story: "That as Alexander was sailing on the Euphrates, and his turban happened to fall off among some reeds, one of his watermen immediately jumped in and swam to it; but as he could not bring it back in his hand without wetting it, he put it upon his head, and so returned with it. Whereupon most historians that have wrote of Alexander (says he) tell us, that he gave him a talent of silver for this expression of his zeal to serve him, but, at the same time, ordered his head to be struck off for presuming to put on the royal diadem." †

When Demaratus, the Lacedæmonian, had been ordered by the king to ask whatsoever he pleased and it should be immediately granted him, he desired that he might make his public entrance into Sardis, and be carried in state through the city with the tiara set in the royal manner upon his head. But the cousin to the king touched him on the head, and told him that he had no brains for the royal tiara to cover, and if Jupiter should give him his lightning and thunder, he would not any the more be Jupiter for that; the king also repulsed him with anger, resolv-

---

* Herodotus, vii, 17.

† Burder, Note in Josephus, *Antiquities.*

ing never to be reconciled to him, but to be inexorable to all supplications on his behalf." *

Of Artaxerxes the following is related: "Teribazus once, when they were hunting, came up and pointed out to the king that his royal robe was torn; the king asked him what he wished him to do; and when Taribazus replied, 'May it please you to put on another and give me that,' the king did so, saying withal, 'I give it you, Teribazus, but I charge you not to wear it.' He, little regarding the injunction, being not a bad, but a light-headed, thoughtless man, immediately the king took it off, put it on, and bedecked himself further with royal golden necklaces and women's ornaments, to the great scandal of every body, the thing being quite unlawful. But the king laughed, and told him, 'You have my leave to wear the trinkets as a woman, and the robe of state as a fool.'" †

It was a large request that Haman presented in behalf of himself. But he felt sure of his ground. He was all-powerful with the king.

What, then, must have been his feelings when the king commanded him to so honor Mordecai! "Make haste, *and* take the apparel and the horse, as thou hast said, and do even so to Mordecai, the Jew, that sitteth at the king's gate: let nothing fail of all that thou hast spoken." Esther vi, 10. "If the king had

---

* Plutarch, *Themistocles*, vol. i. p. 195.

† Plutarch, *Artaxerxes*, vol. iii, pp. 439, 440.

known all his most secret feelings, and had lain on the watch to wound him in the point on which he was most sensitive, and had chosen the most fitting opportunity to make the wound deep beyond endurance, he could not have issued a command so calculated to make Haman writhe under it as this one. And the command at the same time was so peremptory, that he durst not say nay to it."*

The account in the Talmud is purely imaginary, and shows little appreciation of the Persian spirit. Haman is represented as pleading with the king and offering many objections to the proposed honors.

"And Haman answered, 'There are many Jews in Shushan who are called Mordecai; which one is to have the honor?'

"'Do all this that thou hast spoken,' replied the king, 'to Mordecai the Jew who lives by the king's gate; he who hath spoken well to the king and saved his life.'

"When Haman heard these words the blood seemed to congeal in his heart; his face grew blanched, his eyes became dim, and his mouth as though paralyzed; with great effort he said,

"'O king, how—how—can I tell which Mordecai thou meanest?'

"'I have but just said,' returned the king; 'he who dwells at my gate.'

* Davidson.

"'But he hates me,' exclaimed Haman, 'me and my ancestors; do not force me to do him this honor, and I will pay ten thousand silver talents into thy treasury.'

"The king answered, 'Though I should give that ten thousand talents to Mordecai, aye, and give him also thy house to rule over it, yet this honor which thou hast spoken shouldest thou also do to him.'

"'My ten sons shall run before thy chariot,' pleaded Haman; 'they shall be thy slaves, if thou wilt but forego this order.'

"The king answered, 'Though thou and thy wife and thy ten sons should be slaves to Mordecai, yet this honor should be also his.'

"But Haman still entreated. 'Lo, Mordecai is but a common subject of the king. Appoint him ruler of a city, a province, or a street—let that be the honor paid him.'

"And again the king replied: 'Though I should appoint him ruler over all my provinces, though I should cause him to command all who owe me obedience on sea and land, still this honor, too, which thou hast spoken, should be done him. Surely he who has spoken to the advantage of his king, he who has preserved the life of his king, deserves all that should belong to the one whom the king most delights to honor.

"'But the letters,' continued Haman, 'the letters

which have been sent to all thy provinces, condemning him and his people to death.'

"'Peace, peace!' exclaimed the king; 'though they should be recalled, Mordecai should still be honored as thou hast spoken. Say no more, Haman; as thou hast spoken, do quickly; leave out nothing of all that thou hast said.'

"When Haman saw that all appeal was useless, he obeyed the king's orders with a heavy heart." *

Haman knew the king too well to have hesitated for a moment, or to have shown the slightest surprise. He went immediately and procured the royal apparel, and the king's horse with the crown upon his head— "there is seen on Assyrian and old Persian monuments, not so distinct on the latter, horses of the king, and perhaps also of princes, that wear an ornament on their heads terminating in three points, which can easily be taken for a crown"—sought Mordecai, announced the command of the king, placed upon the Jew the royal robe, seated him on the king's horse, brought him through the streets of the city, and proclaimed again and again before him, "Thus shall it be done unto the man whom the king delighteth to honor."

* Polano, *Selections from the Talmud*, pp. 207, 208.

XIV.

POETIC JUSTICE.

"We are sold, I and my people, to be destroyed, to be slain, and to perish."—ESTHER vii, 4.

"Who is he, and where is he, that durst presume in his heart to do so?"—ESTHER vii, 5.

"The adversary and enemy *is* this wicked Haman."—ESTHER vii, 6.

"Behold also the gallows fifty cubits high, which Haman had made for Mordecai."—ESTHER vii, 9.

"Hang him thereon."—ESTHER vii, 9.

MORDECAI returned to his post of duty at the king's gate. Haman hastened to his home, hiding his face so as to avoid recognition, and sought the sympathy of his family and confidential friends. But here he met with a new and unexpected disappointment. Greatly dejected, he recounted to his wife and friends what had befallen him since his departure in the morning. His wise men could discover but an evil omen. They can only say: "If Mordecai *be* of the seed of the Jews, before whom thou hast begun to fall, thou shalt not prevail against him, but shalt surely fall before him." There was no time for consultation. There was no time to form any plans. Destiny rushes storming on. "And while they *were* yet talking with him, came the king's chamberlains, and hasted to bring Haman unto the banquet that Esther had prepared." He went, but not "merrily." Esther vi, 13, 14.

At the feast every thing looks propitious for Haman. The king becomes unusually merry, feeds the pride of Haman, and is ready to bestow upon him every honor. The queen is modest, attractive, beautiful, and entertaining, and smiles sweetly. Surely his position and standing with the king and queen are secure. All will soon be bright again. He will yet be avenged upon his enemy. The cloud disappears from his mind. He is merry.

Again, for the third time, the king asked: "What *is* thy petition, Queen Esther? and it shall be granted thee: and what *is* thy request? and it shall be performed, *even* to the half of the kingdom." The curiosity of Xerxes was excited, and she could not trifle with his anxiety to know her desire. She had more than regained her place in his affections. He was ready to grant her request. This was her opportunity. Her lips are at last unsealed. She speaks, and speaks directly to the point. There are in her words the skill of earnestness and the art of artlessness. In two burning sentences she tells the whole truth. She petitions for her own life and that of her people. If they had been condemned only to be sold into slavery she would have held her peace, although were the enemy to exhaust all his resources the king would have been the loser. But she cannot be silent when she and her people have been sold to destroy, to kill, and to cause to perish. She uses the very words of the infamous decree. There can be no mistaking her meaning.

Her nationality is revealed. The king sees what he has done. He is aroused and excited. "He throws out his pronouns in a wild confusion of excitement, and then repeats them with the order inverted. 'Who is he, that one—and where is that one, he, whose heart has filled him (with the audacity) to do so?'— it is clear that the identification cannot wait. It must be prompt and unmistakable. And the queen is equal to the demand. The queen's blood is up. She sees her advantage; and she speaks with all the vehemence of one who has deeply felt the monstrous injustice of Haman's plot. The collocation of the words in the Hebrew leaves no doubt that they were accompanied with a gesture of the hand; her scorn and righteous indignation flashed out, as it were, at her very finger's-end, as she pointed to him. 'The man, adversary, and enemy, is Haman, the wretch, this (one).' Well might he be terror-stricken in that presence. He reads, in the king's countenance and in his movements, the angry excitement that has taken possession of him." *

It is a thunder-clap from a clear sky. His favorite

---

* The Lowell Hebrew Club, *The Book of Esther*, p. 69.

minister of state, whom he has raised to a position of unexampled dignity and power, has betrayed his confidence. His matchless queen stands upon the crumbling brink of a volcanic crater. A nation of peaceable, law-abiding, and industrious citizens has been doomed to slaughter. He himself has been led to give his royal sanction to the wicked and nefarious plot. The king rises from the table in uncontrollable anger, and goes out into the garden of the palace, not so much to cool his wrath as to collect his thoughts. He walks back and forth in the vain endeavor to control the whirlwind of passion that rages within his breast. The atrocity of the intended massacre grows upon him, and his soul is set on fire.

Haman has no hope in the king. Perhaps the heart of the queen can be moved. He pleads before her for his life. His case is most desperate. The moments are precious. He pleads more earnestly. In a frenzy of despair he bows his head upon the couch where the queen reclines at the banquet. In his agony of deadly fear he catches hold upon her robe, and embraces her feet.

The king returns from the garden. He sees Haman in the attitude of supplication at the feet of the queen. The pent-up fires of his wrath must burst forth. Can it be that Haman hopes to force the queen to yield to his petition, and thus save his life, by the very anguish of his mortal terror? The thought feeds his rage. The commandment—not "the word," (the Hebrew *dabhar* is rendered "commandment" eight times in the Book of Esther)—the commandment went forth from the king's mouth. It was Haman's condemnation, and the king's attendants cover his face. He is no longer worthy to behold the light of day.

When the last of the Horatii returned from his conquest, carrying the spoils of the Curiatii, "his sister, a maiden who had been betrothed to one of the Curiatii, met him before the gate Capena, and having recognized her lover's military robe, which she herself had wrought, on her brother's shoulders, she tore her hair, and with bitter wailings called by name on her deceased lover. The sister's lamentations in the midst of his own victory, and of such great public rejoicings, raised the indignation of the excited youth. Having, therefore, drawn his sword, he ran the damsel through the body, at the same time chiding her in these words: 'Go hence with thy unseasonable love to thy spouse, forgetful of thy dead brothers, and of him who survives; forgetful of thy native country. So perish every Roman woman who shall mourn an enemy.' This action seemed shocking to the fathers and to the people; but his recent services outweighed its guilt. Nevertheless he was carried before the king for judgment. The king, that he himself might not be the author of a decision so melancholy, and so disagreeable to the people, or of the punishment consequent on that decision, having summoned an assembly of the people, says, 'I appoint, according to law, duumvirs to pass sentence on Horatius for treason.' The law was of dreadful import. 'Let the duumvirs pass sentence for treason. If he appeal from the duumvirs, let him contend by appeal; if they shall gain the cause, cover his head; hang him by a rope from a gallows; scourge him either within the Pomoerium or without the Pomoerium.' When the duumvirs appointed by this law, who did not consider that, according to law, they could acquit even an innocent person, had found him guilty, one of them says, 'P. Horatius, I judge thee guilty of treason. Go, lictor, bind his hands.' The lictor had approached him, and was fixing the rope. Then Horatius, by the advice of Tullus, a favorable interpreter of the law, says, 'I appeal.' Accordingly, the matter was contested by appeal to the people. On that trial persons were much affected, especially by P. Horatius, the father, declaring that he considered his daughter deservedly slain; were it not so, that he would, by his authority as a father have inflicted punishment on his son. He then entreated that they would not render childless him whom but a little while ago they had beheld with a fine progeny. During these words the old man, having embraced the youth, pointing to the spoils of the Curiatii fixed up in that place which is now called Pila Horatia, 'Romans,' said he, 'can you bear to see bound beneath a gallows, amidst scourges and tortures, him whom you just now beheld marching decorated (with spoils) and exulting in victory; a sight so shocking as the eyes even of the Albans could scarcely endure. Go, lictor; bind those hands which but a little while since, being armed, established sovereignty for the Roman people. Go, cover the head of the liberator of this city; hang him on the gallows; scourge him, either within the Pomoerium, so it be only amidst those javelins and spoils of the enemy; or without the Pomoerium, only amidst the graves of the Curiatii. For whither can you bring this youth, where his own glories must not redeem him from such ignominy of punishment.' The people could not withstand the tears of the father or the resolution of the son, so undaunted in every danger; and acquitted him more through admiration of his bravery than for the justice of his cause. But that so notorious a murder might be atoned for by some expiation, the father was commanded to make satisfaction for the son at the public charge. He, having offered certain expiatory sacrifices, which were ever after continued in the Horatian family, and laid a beam across the street, made his son pass under it as under a yoke, with his head covered." *

* Livy, i, 26.

To cover the head was to begin to execute the sentence. "Philetas—with covered head they brought into the palace."* "Go, lictor, bind his hands, cover his head, hang him on the hapless tree." †

The suggestion of Harbonah came just at the right time; "Behold also the gallows fifty cubits high, which Haman had made for Mordecai, standeth in the house of Haman." The object of Harbonah may have been merely to point to another evidence of Haman's murderous spirit. The king, however, thought of something further. He commanded sternly, "Hang him thereon." The sentence is quickly executed. Haman is hurried away, and on the gallows erected for Mordecai, high in air, seen by all the inhabitants of Shushan, hangs the lifeless body of the enemy and adversary of the Jews. "Then was the king's wrath pacified."

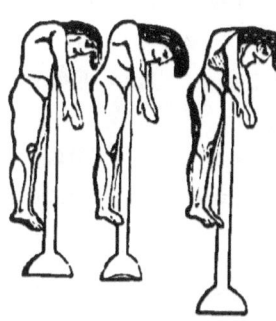

IMPALEMENT.

*Quintus Curtius, vi, 8, 22. † Cicero, *Pro C. Rabirio*, iv, 13.

XV.

THE BEGINNING OF THE END.

"And the king took off his ring, which he had taken from Haman, and gave it unto Mordecai."—ESTHER viii, 2.

"The king granted the Jews . . . to stand for their life."—ESTHER viii, 11.

"The city of Shushan rejoiced and was glad."—ESTHER viii, 15.

"The Jews had joy and gladness, a feast and a good day."—ESTHER viii, 17.

UPON the execution of a criminal his property was confiscated to the crown, according to law. Cyrus, in his instructions to the governors that were in Syria, said: "My will is, that those who disobey these instructions, and make them void, shall be hung upon a cross, and their substance brought into the king's treasury." * When Oroetes was slain at the command of Darius, his treasures were conveyed to the king at Sardis.† Even when a great man was dismissed in disgrace his property was forfeited to the crown.

So, on that very day, the king gave Haman's property to Esther. The queen now informed Xerxes of her relationship to Mordecai, and what kindness and care he had shown her as her guardian and foster-parent. The king recognized him as a man of

---

* Josephus, *Antiquities*, xi, 1, 3; 4, 6.   † Herodotus, iii, 129.

worth, and made him the first minister of state. The signet-ring, which had been taken from the hand of Haman, the king gave to Mordecai, while Esther appointed him administrator of the property of the enemy and adversary of the Jews.

Haman is indeed dead, but the influence of his life remains. The decree of extermination is still in force against the Jews throughout the whole empire. Something more must be done. The newly-created prime minister does not feel sure of his influence with the king. Esther must again intercede. She ventures into the royal presence. She does not present her petition in the same manner as formerly. She is now pleading for others. The strain upon her mind and heart has been so great and so long continued that she cannot maintain her former composure. Her womanly tenderness, queenly interest and Christian affection can find expression only in tears. With a heart bleeding for her people she came to the king, "and fell down at his feet, and besought him with tears to put away the mischief of Haman the Agagite, and his device that he had devised against the Jews"— "the machination which he machinated." "The Hebrew language has no stronger word to imply that Haman, a man of great powers, put his whole thought and ingenuity into the plot of ruining the people of God." *

* Greene.

The king extended to her the golden scepter as a pledge of favor, and she arose and stood before him and said: " If it please the king, and if I have found favor in his sight, and the thing *seem* right before the king, and I *be* pleasing in his eyes, let it be written to reverse the letters devised by Haman the son of Hammedatha the Agagite, which he wrote to destroy the Jews which *are* in all the king's provinces: for how can I endure to see the evil that shall come unto my people? or how can I endure to see the destruction of my kindred?" Esther viii. 5, 6.

This address shows a noble and truly heroic soul. Every respect is shown the king, and she petitions only in subordination to his own personal judgment. She is careful not to charge the king with an injustice. The letters were " devised by Haman." " He wrote " the edict of butchery. The king has already passed judgment on the murderous plot in condemning Haman. He may now complete the work and reverse, by his higher authority, the edict of slaughter devised by his subordinate. And now the gentle heart of the woman is shown: " How can I endure to see the evil that shall come unto my people? or how can I endure to see the destruction of my kindred?"

"This verse is the irrepressible outcry of true patriotism. It is the expostulation of vivid and tender sympathy. It is the argument of a forcible principle of our nature, which oversteps the boundaries of the personal and the domestic in order to travel much further and to embrace the national. It mounts by the stepping-stones of self-love and sacred family love to the love of vast numbers of those never seen nor personally known, yet in some special sense related." *

The king answers that he has already done enough to convince her of his favorable disposition. He has executed Haman and has presented her with his vast estate; and this because Haman sought the destruction of the Jews. The decree cannot be recalled, because it was sealed with the king's seal and is hence virtually his own. Something, however, may be done toward its mitigation. He grants to Mordecai and the queen authority to devise some plan, and to issue letters in his name and seal them with his seal. They may adopt any plan which they can devise, provided only they allow the decree of extermination to stand. The fiction of his divine character, and hence infallibility, must be maintained. There must not be the slightest breath of suspicion that THE KING may possibly make a mistake. The laws of the Medes and Persians change not.

We have noted the many difficulties connected with this principle.

"A Persian king who reigned not very many years ago—Aga Mahmed Khan—having set out upon

* Barker.

a military expedition, and encamped in a place convenient for his purpose, gave forth his edict that the encampment should not be removed until the snow had disappeared from the neighboring mountains. The season was severe. The snow clung to the mountains longer than usual, and in the meantime the army became straitened for supplies. Here was an unexpected difficulty. The king's appointment must stand, but the result was likely to be ruinous. To avert the difficulty, then, a vast multitude of laborers were despatched to clear away as far as they could the snow that was visible from the camp; and with their aid and the help of a few days of sunshine the snow disappeared, and then immediately the army was put in motion." *

At that very time Mordecai summoned the king's scribes. They wrote letters to the satraps and pashas, or the principal and subordinate imperial civil magistrates of the provinces; to the deputies or native local officers; and to the Jews, who were not addressed in the former edict—to each nation in its own written alphabet and spoken dialect. It was the twenty-third day of the third month, the month Sivan.

The month Sivan is devoted to Sin, the moon-god, and corresponds to May–June. In the symbolic and religious nomenclature it is "the month of brick-

* Davidson, *Lectures on Esther*, p. 266.

making" in which an old ritual ordained the liturgic ceremony to be observed for the molding of bricks for sacred buildings and royal edifices. "Religion in this case consecrated a usage resulting from the physical climatic conditions. In Chaldea and Babylonia the majority of the edifices were built of bricks simply dried in the sun. The third month of the year* coincides with the period when the waters of the Euphrates and Tigris, which have been rising during March and April, begin to fall; the condition of the soil left by the retreating waters makes it easy to mold the bricks at that particular time, and then to have them dry in the sun, already burning in its heat, though not yet fierce enough to crack the raw brick, which would inevitably happen if they were dried in July or August."† Inasmuch as the building of the first city is connected with the first fratricide, this month is called "the month of the twins," and Lenormant thinks that it is also symbolic of that primeval tragedy.

So the letters were written, and sealed with the king's seal, and hastened with all despatch to all the provinces of the empire by special couriers mounted upon the most swift and famous coursers. Had it not been for these letters the Jews would have been expected to remain passive while their enemies slew

* Sivan, May–June.
† Lenormant, *Beginnings of History*, pp. 147, 148.

them, but they are now authorized to defend themselves against violence and death. The support and protection of the government are withdrawn from any who venture by the authority of the former edict to attack the Jews, while the whole power of the government is pledged to protect the Jews in their struggle of self-defense. They may assemble, organize, and prepare for the thirteenth day of the month Adar. Since the edict of slaughter extended only to that one day, the present edict protects them only when their lives would be in danger. Any attempt upon their lives upon any other day would be unlawful.

ORDINARY PERSIAN COSTUME.

It is probable that much of the Book of Esther is drawn from the official records of the kingdom, and that we have the very words of the decree: "To assemble and stand for their lives; to destroy, to kill, and to cause to perish all the force of people and province assailing them; [to destroy] little children and women, and [take] their property for spoil, in one day, throughout all the provinces of the king

Xerxes; on the thirteenth of the twelfth month, that is, the month Adar." The terms of this edict are as comprehensive as those of the former. The scribes certified the writing: "A copy of the writing to be given as a decree in every province, published to all the peoples; even for the Jews to be ready on that day to be avenged on their enemies." *

With earnestness and resolution the king has espoused the cause of the Jews. The decree was doubtless submitted to the king for his inspection and approval, for the posts were hastened and pressed on by his commandment.

The month Adar is sacred to the seven great gods, and symbolizes "the deposit of seed time," and is historically connected with the return to the cultivation of the earth after the great deluge. The zodiacal sign of this month—the fish—perpetuates the memory of the salvation of the righteous from the Noachian flood.

Mordecai was now clad in the suitable dress of the prime minister—"in royal apparel of blue and white, and with a great crown of gold, and with a robe of fine linen and purple."—R. V. The Persian monarch himself wore a purple robe and an inner vest of purple striped with white.† The robes of honor which he gave away were of many different colors,

---

* The Lowell Hebrew Club, *The Book of Esther*, pp. 77, 78.

† Rawlinson, *Ancient Monarchies*, vol. iii, pp. 202, 203.

but generally of a single tint throughout;* but the one given to Mordecai seems to have been blue with white stripes. These were the colors of the royal diadem.† The golden crown was not the kingly diadem, but such a crown as might be worn by the greatest nobles. How soon has sackcloth been exchanged for goodly apparel!

"The city of Shushan shouted and was glad."— R. V. When the former decree was issued, "the city Shushan was perplexed."

Haman was an accomplished courtier, a profusive flatterer, a skillful diplomatist, a wise financier, a successful politician, a royal favorite, and a man fertile in expedients, yet the success of his administration of the government was only in appearance. An Oriental despotism would tolerate little unfavorable criticism, but the story of his career leaves no doubt that his acts were offensive to the people. He had, indeed, powerful and influential friends, but neither officially nor socially did he command sincere respect. While his influence was dominant in the capital, the city was perplexed, and there was, doubtless, little mourning at his death.

The large majority of the Persians seem to have been friendly to the Jews. Their religion had many points in contact with that of the exiles. The real

---

* Xen., *Cyrop.*, viii, 3, § 3.

† Rawlinson, Q. Curt., *Vit. Alex*, iii, 3.

enemies of the Jews were among the distinctively heathen nations.

It augured well for the new administration of Mordecai that his first measure was popular and received the enthusiastic support of his people. Happy the ruler whose influence and authority are anchored in the popular heart. The city of Shushan rejoiced.

And especially to the Jews there were "light, and gladness, and joy, and honor." Not only was this true of the Jews dwelling in Shushan, but as this new decree of the king was published throughout all the provinces of the empire, "whithersoever the king's commandment and his decree came the Jews had joy and gladness, a feast and a good day." Since the queen and the prime minister belonged to the Jewish race, and the king himself was well disposed and had issued a favorable decree, and since the hand of Providence was so manifest in their history, the fear of the Jews fell upon the people, and doubtless many feared their God, and, as a consequence, not a few, either for prudential reasons or from conscientious motives, became proselytes to their faith. Persecution resulted in the spiritual and numerical growth of the Church.

What a multitude of events have been crowded into a single day! What a change has been wrought in the interests of the people of God! The sleepless night, the reading of the records of the kingdom, the story of the conspiracy against the life of Xerxes, his awakened conscience, the early visit of Haman to obtain an order for the execution of Mordecai, the prime minister summoned into the royal presence, the question proposed, the self-conceit of the grand vizier, the answer to the king's question, the honor conferred upon Mordecai, the humiliation and vexation of the royal favorite, the dark forebodings of his wife and his wise men, the queen's banquet, "What is thy petition, Queen Esther?" the charge against Haman, the king's wrath, the first minister of state pleading for his life, his condemnation and execution upon the gallows erected for Mordecai, the confiscation of his property and its presentation to Esther, her appointment of Mordecai over the estate, his elevation to the office of prime minister, Esther's second petition, the publication of the counter-edict throughout the provinces, joy in Shushan and among all the Jews—enough, surely, for one day.

XVI.

VICTORY, PEACE, GLADNESS.

"The Jews gathered themselves together in their cities throughout all the provinces."—ESTHER ix, 2.

"The Jews smote all their enemies."—ESTHER ix, 5.

"Days of feasting and joy, and of sending portions one to another, and gifts to the poor."—ESTHER ix, 22.

ON the thirteenth day of the first month the decree of slaughter was sent forth; on the twenty-third day of the third month a decree was issued permitting the Jews to stand in self-defense; and the thirteenth day of the twelfth month was fixed for the execution of the bloody decree. Nearly nine months gave the Jews ample time to complete their preparation for self-defense.

In any modern and civilized government a proclamation might have been made, setting forth that the former decree had been procured upon false information, declaring it void, and forbidding all persons slaying or injuring the Jews or interfering with their property. But the peculiar Persian constitution did not permit the use of common sense. Whatever passed the royal signet could not be reversed, not even by the monarch himself. The former decree was still in force. It was lawful to destroy the Jewish nation, so that any one who murdered a Jew or seized his property was secure against punishment. The second decree made it lawful for the Jews to defend themselves, so that any Jew who slew an enemy or seized his property was secure against punishment. It was a proclamation of legalized civil war, a species of judicial combat.

Had this second edict not been issued the Jews would doubtless in many cases have stood for their lives. The right and duty of self-defense for self-preservation would have been their sufficient justification. A divine instinct, more commanding than all human law, would have stirred them to fight for their lives wherever their numbers raised them above contempt.

But the edict permitting them to defend themselves gave them two important advantages. They could prepare for the struggle by gathering together in their villages and strongholds and thoroughly organizing, and the co-operation and protection of the government were withdrawn from their enemies.

The decree in behalf of the Jews was as wide in its application as the former decree. Each permitted the slaying of women and children and their seizure of property. The Jews, however, were only to defend themselves against attack and slay those who sought their hurt. But why did not this second decree prevent the war? The enemies of the Jews—largely among the heathen tribes—had often threatened the Jews and reminded them of the day of their doom. They had more than once told them that they were only waiting for the thirteenth day of the month Adar, when they would sweep the whole race from the face of the earth. They had gone too far to retreat. They had also stirred the wrath of the Jews, and feared their vengeance.

The day came, and the Jews assembled in those cities where their numbers were greatest. Their enemies rushed to the attack, but the Jews were mightier than their mightiest foes, and no man could successfully face the people of God. They were also assisted by the government, for " all the rulers of the provinces, and the lieutenants, and the deputies, and officers of the king, helped the Jews; because the fear of Mordecai fell upon all. . . . Thus the Jews smote all their enemies with the stroke of the sword, and slaughter, and destruction." Their courage and united efforts, with the encouragement and assistance of the rulers and the blessing of God, brought them victory.

The population of Shushan at this time has been estimated at five hundred thousand souls, and the population of the whole Persian empire at one hundred million. On the day of judicial combat five hundred men were slain in "Shushan the palace" and seventy-five thousand in the empire outside the capital. This may be but a rough estimate quickly made from the reports already received. It was the custom in their final reports to make out and record the numbers with extreme exactness. The losses sustained by the Jews, if any there were, are not mentioned.

The enemies of the Jews were doubtless idolaters and not Persians. Foremost among these in Shushan were the intimate friends of Haman, who may have been under the immediate leadership of his ten sons, with whom the struggle was most desperate. The writer exultantly records their names—Parshandatha, Dalphon, Aspatha, Poratha, Adalia, Aridatha, Parmashta, Arisai, Aridai, and Vajezatha. These names, except Adalia, are readily traceable to Persian roots. It is interesting to note the meanings of these Persian names of a noble and warlike family — "Given to Persia," "Arrogant," "Horseman," "Having many Chariots," "Liberal," "Very Greatest," "Mighty Conqueror," "Free Giver," and "Strong as the Wind." Haman had determined to destroy the whole Jewish race. God so overruled in the affairs of men that the Jews were victorious, and the ten sons of Haman, who were his boast and pride, were slain.

The Jews acted on the defensive, and hence slew only the armed force of the people. The edict permitted them " to destroy, to kill, and cause to perish little children and women," but the history expressly states that they put to death only men. The edict also permitted them to seize the property of their enemies, but three times it is emphatically declared, " on the spoil they laid not their hands." This is an honor to their religion, wisdom, and humanity, and shows that morally they occupied a far higher position than their enemies.

The day of conflict is drawing to a close. The number of the slain has been reported to the king. His interest in the cause of the Jews increases, and his anxiety to save and protect them quickens his foresight and decision. He sees that their heathen foes will be driven to more desperate efforts by their uncontrollable rage. He believes that in "Shushan the palace," where the friends of Haman are most bitter, the Jews will need still further protection. He is not sure of the course which he ought to pursue. He will ask Esther: "And the king said unto Esther the queen, The Jews have slain and destroyed five hundred men in Shushan the palace, and the ten sons of Haman; what have they done in the rest of the king's provinces? Now what *is* thy petition? and it shall be granted thee: or what *is* thy request further? and it shall be done." Esther ix, 12.

The queen had doubtless consulted with Mordecai and other influential Jews who understood the situation and were qualified to advise with full personal knowledge of the need. She asks that the privilege of self-defense may be extended to another day, and that the bodies of the ten sons of Haman may be impaled. The former request being granted, they can defend themselves against attack; the impalement of the bodies of the ten sons of Haman will strike terror into their enemies and, possibly, prevent any further effusion of blood. The king grants these reasonable requests. The history of the next day proves their wisdom. The Jews are again attacked, and slay three hundred of their enemies who seek their lives; "but on the spoil they laid not their hands."

The crisis over, and the danger past, the Jews rest from their troubles and anxiety, and spend a day of "feasting and gladness." The Jews of Shushan, because of the two days' struggle, celebrated the fifteenth of Adar, while "the Jews of the villages, that dwelt in the unwalled towns, made the fourteenth day of the month Adar *a day* of gladness and feasting, and a good day, and of sending portions one to another." The celebration was spontaneous. "No words can describe the solicitude and fear which must have filled the Jews in anticipation of the dreadful day fixed upon for their destruction. But now it was all over; God had appeared as their helper, and their troubles were at an end. Sweet deliverance and rest were now their portion. In commemoration of their happy state on this day, they made it a day of 'feasting and gladness.' They did not celebrate the slaughter. There was no reminder of the day on which the destruction of their enemies occurred; but the days on which rest and quiet came to them had a lasting memorial." *

Mordecai at once recognized the appropriateness and importance of celebrating, by an annual festival, their providential deliverance and rest. To secure uniformity throughout the empire, he sent letters enjoining upon the Jews to celebrate both the fourteenth and the fifteenth of Adar. He seems to have accompanied his recommendation by a history of the great struggle through which his people had passed. To keep alive their sense of gratitude to God for his signal providence the days were to be observed not only as days of joy and gladness, but also as days of good feeling, benevolence, and charity — " days of feasting and gladness, and sending portions every one to his neighbor, and gifts to the poor."

The Jews adopted the recommendation of Mordecai. "Now, because of all the words of this letter, and of what they had seen concerning the matter, and what had come to them, the Jews ordained, and took upon themselves, and upon their children, and upon all who should join themselves to them, without fail to keep these two days according to the

* Greene.

writing in respect to them, and according to the time appointed for them each year; that these days should be remembered and kept in every generation, every family, every province, and every city; and that these days of Purim should not fail from the midst of the Jews, nor the memorial of them perish from their race." Esther ix, 26-28.

The queen was deeply interested in this festival. Such were the anxieties, trials, dangers, and agonies through which she had passed that she felt impelled to prepare another letter, which was sent to all the Jews of the one hundred and twenty and seven provinces, which, with messages of "peace and truth," enjoined upon them "with all authority" the observance of these days. This "second letter" ordained fasting and crying—"the fasting and their cry"—in connection with Purim. It is probable that the thirteenth of Adar was the day appointed for this fasting, humiliation, and prayer. It would keep vividly before them the awful peril and the mighty deliverance, and would prepare them for the profitable observance of the days of feasting and gladness. It would commemorate both Esther's fasting before going to the king and the dark day of terror and slaughter. Posssibly this day of fasting was originally suggested to the popular heart, and Esther and Mordecai, as was the case in the former edict, merely followed the indications of Providence. This second letter, called "the edict of Esther," since it originated with her, was written in the "book," and hence in the highest sense became official.

Haman cast lots to determine an auspicious day upon which to carry out the bloody decree obtained through his influence against the Jews. In irony the festival which commemorates the deliverance of the Jews is called Lots, or Purim. If the fourteenth happens on the Sabbath, or on the second or fourth day of the week, the festival is deferred till the next day. Jewish tradition says that eighty-five Jewish elders objected to the institution of Purim when it was first proposed by Mordecai. This is quite improbable. If the thirteenth of Adar is the Sabbath, the fast of Esther is held on the fifth day of the week. It cannot be held on the sixth, since dishes prepared for the Sabbath must be tasted.

Purim is still celebrated by the Jews. On the fourteenth of Adar, as soon as the stars begin to appear, candles are lighted in token of rejoicing, and the people assemble in the synagogue. The religious exercises begin with prayer and thanksgiving. The Book of Esther, written in a peculiar manner, and called in pre-eminence "The Roll," is now read. The text is translated into the tongue of the people and explained. Whenever the reader pronounces the name of Haman the whole congregation, remembering the king's edict of extermination, with true Jewish spirit, cry out, "Let his name be blotted out; may the name of the wicked rot;" while the children, with equal vehemence, hiss, make a noise with their hands, strike the wall with mallets, and strike together blocks of wood or pieces of stone, upon which they have written the name of Haman, so as to rub out the writing. The names of Haman's ten sons are written in three perpendicular columns, as they are said to have hung on the stake. The Targum of Esther says that they all hung in one line, Haman at the top, and his sons under him at regular intervals of half a cubit. It is said further that Zeresh and the seventy remaining sons fled, and were compelled to beg their bread from door to door. When the names of the ten sons of Haman are read they are pronounced in one breath, to express the belief that they all perished at one instant. When the reading is finished the congregation exclaim: "Cursed be Haman; blessed be Mordecai; cursed be Zeresh; blessed be Esther; cursed be all idolaters; blessed be all Israelites; and blessed be Harbonah who hanged Haman."

All now return to their homes and partake of a meal composed principally of eggs and milk. On the second day of the festival, after the prayers in the synagogue, the passages of Scripture which relate to the destruction of the Amalekites are read; and then again the Book of Esther, as on the previous day. All are required to hear the reading on these days. Even cripples, invalids, and idiots are not excused, so important is the service considered by every true Israelite.

When the service of the synagogue is over, all give themselves to merry-making. They play various games, and dance, while music enlivens the festivities. Frequently dramatic entertainments add to the pleasure of the occasion. They are also at liberty to disregard the rules in regard to dress, and each sex may appear in the attire of the other. Gifts are exchanged, and the poor are not forgotten. It is written in the Talmud that at the feast of Purim a man should drink till he cannot tell the words "Cursed be Haman" from "Blessed be Mordecai." It is certain, however, that the modern Jews, at least, observe the feast with sobriety and temperance. The estimation in which Purim has been held may be seen from several proverbs. They say, "The Temple may fail, but Purim never." "The Prophets may fail, but not the Megillah;" "The Roll," or Book of Esther, read at the festival.

Ezra and Nehemiah mention one Mordecai who was one of the leaders of the captives who returned from Babylon to Judea, and Josephus says that one Mordecai was an ambassador to king Darius from the Jews.

Ctesias, who claims to have had access to the official

chronicles of Media and Persia, mentions one Matacas or Natacas, a most powerful favorite of Xerxes, and some authors have identified him with Mordecai. When Megabysus refused to plunder the temple of Apollo at Delphi, Xerxes sent Matacas, who insulted the god, plundered the temple, and thereby fully satisfied the king. It has been thought that Xerxes would readily have selected as his prime minister one whose hatred of idolatry would have specially qualified him for carrying out the iconoclastic ideas of the Persian king.

XVII.

PROSPERITY, HAPPINESS.

"For Mordecai the Jew *was* next unto king Ahasuerus, and great among the Jews, and accepted of the multitude of his brethren, seeking the wealth of his people, and speaking peace to all his seed."— ESTHER x, iii.

DARIUS, after taking possession of the Persian government, " proceeded to establish twenty governments of the kind which the Persians call satrapies, assigning to each its governor, and fixing the tribute which was to be paid him by the several nations. And generally he joined together in one satrapy the nations that were neighbors, but sometimes he passed over the nearer tribes, and put in their stead those which were more remote. . . . The whole revenue which came in to Darius year by year will be found to be, in Euboic money, fourteen thousand five hundred and sixty talents, not to mention parts of a talent"—an equivalent, in our time, to about two hundred and sixty-two million five hundred thousand dollars.

"Such was the revenue which Darius derived from Asia and a small part of Libya. Later in his reign the sum was increased by the tribute of the islands and of the nations of Europe as far as Thessaly. The great king stores away the tribute which he receives after this fashion—he melts it down, and while it is in a liquid state runs it into earthen vessels, which are afterward removed, leaving the metal in a solid mass. When money is wanted, he coins as much of this bullion as the occasion requires."

The country of the Persians was altogether exempt from taxes. The Ethiopians and their neighbors on the borders of Egypt were not taxed, but brought gifts to the king. "Every third year these two nations brought—and they still bring, to my day—two choenices of virgin gold, two hundred logs of ebony, five Ethiopian boys, and twenty elephant tusks. The Colchians, and the neighboring tribes who dwell between them and the Caucasus—for so far the Persian rule reaches, while north of the Caucasus no one fears them any longer—undertook to furnish a gift, which in my day was still brought every fifth year, consisting of a hundred boys, and the same number of maidens. The Arabs brought every year a thousand talents of frankincense. Such were the gifts which the king received over and above the tribute-money."*

The rivers of the empire, fisheries, and probably other possessions were crown property, and yielded large revenues to the state.†

* Herodotus, iii, 89, 95, 96, 97.   † *Ibid.*, iii, 117.

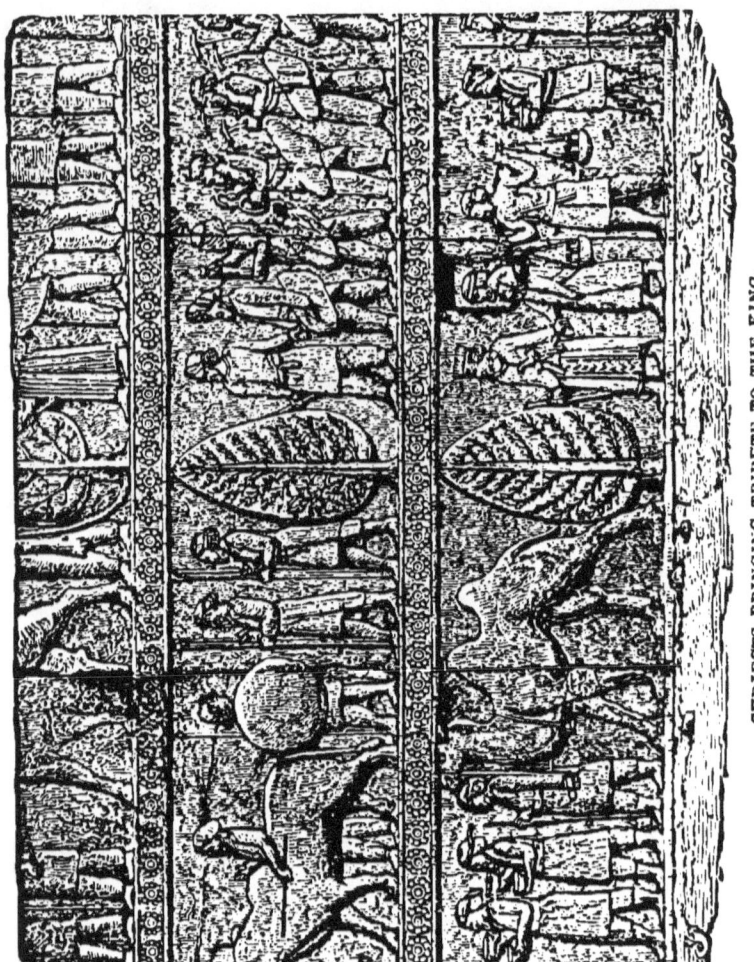

SUBJECTS BRINGING TRIBUTE TO THE KING.

Governors were appointed to the satrapies by the king, and were removed or executed at his pleasure. Their chief duty was to collect and transmit to the capital the tribute. This tribute was only for the royal court. The satraps and other officers must look after their own compensation.

"As they represented the monarch, their courts were framed upon the royal model; they had their palaces, surrounded by magnificent parks and hunting grounds—their numerous train of eunuchs and attendants, and their own household troops or bodyguard. They assessed the tribute on the several towns and villages within their jurisdiction at their pleasure, and appointed deputies, called sometimes, like themselves, satraps, over cities or districts within their province, whose office was regarded as one of great dignity. So long as they were in favor at court, they ruled their satrapies with an absolute sway, involving no little tyranny and oppression. Besides the fixed tribute which each satrap was obliged to remit to the king, and the amount that he had to collect for the payment of the troops of his province, he might exact, for his own personal expenses and the support of his court, whatever sum he considered his province able to furnish. All persons who had any favor, or even justice, to ask approached him with gifts, without which success was not to be looked for; and hence enormous fortunes were accumulated. The sole limit upon the rapacity of the satrap was the fear of removal in case the voice of complaint became so loud as to reach the ears of the monarch."*

The inhabitants of those provinces through which the king led his armies gave him many valuable presents.

This system, though a great improvement on the more ancient financial plan of the Assyrian and Babylonian courts, was liable to abuse. The people often suffered under the despotic hand of oppression. Property was insecure, and motives to industry and frugality were few. The resources of the empire could be but imperfectly developed.

Xerxes made a new assessment of the tribute required for the expenses of his court—tribute of personal service, money, and the productions of the provinces. This tribute he laid both upon the land and upon the islands of the sea — Cyprus, Aradus, the island of Tyre, the maritime tracts of Europe which were occupied by Persian garrisons, and possibly the islands of the Ægean, whose independence he would be slow to recognize.† Special efforts would be required to replenish the treasury exhausted by his Grecian campaigns. Mordecai seconded the king in this work. Although next to the king he was not

---

* Rawlinson, *Herodotus*, vol. ii, p. 462.

† Herodotus, vii, 106, 107.

forgetful of his own people, for he was "great among the Jews, and accepted of the multitude of his brethren, seeking the wealth of his people, and speaking peace to all his seed," or to all the Jewish people. "He was not a dumb man, never having any thing to say for God or the Church; but one of his distinguishing characteristics was that he spoke peace to his race. Peace is one of the grandest and sweetest words in the Hebrew language. It was used in salutations. "Peace be to you," was the Jewish benediction. Peace means welfare, health, prosperity, and all that is good. Mordecai was not a fault-finder, a censurer, but he spoke words of cheer, hope, encouragement, and prosperity to his race." *

The rabbis have ever honored the memory of Mordecai. They have praised him in terms of extravagant exaggeration. They say that he knew the seventy languages of the nations of the tenth chapter of Genesis. They surname him, and we believe with good reason, The Just. They describe in ample terms his splendid robes, his Persian buskins, and his Median scymetars. They describe the golden crown which he wore, the rich profusion of precious stones and Macedonian gold on which they said there was an engraved view of Jerusalem, and the phylacteries over the crown. They relate how myrtle boughs were strewed in the streets along which he passed. They

* Greene.

speak with pride of his numerous attendants, the heralds with their trumpets, and the great glory and exaltation of his people.

The so-called tomb of Modecai and Esther, a place of unusal interest, is at Hamadan or Ecbatana. "The tomb stands on ground somewhat more elevated than

THE TOMB OF MORDECAI AND ESTHER.

any in the immediate neighborhood, and is in rather a decayed condition. It occupies a small space in the midst of ruins, in the quarter appropriated to Jewish families. The entrance to the building is by a stone door of small dimensions, the key of which is always kept by the chief rabbi. This door conducts to the antechamber, which is larger than the outer apartment. In the midst of this stand the two sarcophagi of Mordecai and Esther, of dark and hard wood, like that of Ezra. They are cenotaphs, standing beside each other, distinguished only by the one (Mordecai's) being a little larger than the other. They are richly carved, and have a Hebrew inscription along the upper ledge, taken from Esther ii, 5, and x, 3."

"The wood is in good preservation, though evidently very old. The present building is said to occupy the site of one more magnificent, which was destroyed by Timur Beg, soon after which this humble building was erected in its place, at the expense of certain devout Jews; and it is added that it was fully repaired about one hundred and sixty years since by a rabbi named Ismael. If this local statement be correct, some of the inscriptions which now appear must, as the resident Jews state, have belonged to the preceding building, which, however, could not have been the *original* mausoleum, since one of these inscriptions describes it as having been finished posterior to the Christian Era."

The apocryphal additions to the Book of Esther are by a later hand and possess little value. The author of the canonical work drew from the official records of the kingdom to which he refers for more complete historical information. These original records have been lost, but their former existence is without question.

The name of God is not mentioned in this whole book, but his providence, his power, his grace, and his love for the people are manifest in every line.

INDEX.

Aaron, 149.
Abehail, 116.
Abib, 166.
Abigail, 150.
Abraham entertains angels, 46.
Acanthians, 207.
Accadians, 15, 26, 27, 160.
Adar, 231.
Advisers, the king's, 90, 91.
    decision of, 92-95.
Æschylus, 150, 179.
Aga Mahmed Khan, 227, 228.
Agag, 150.
Ahasuerus, 16.
    character fits Xerxes, 22.
    chronology of events, 23.
    transliteration of name, 22.
Ahinoam, 150.
Ahuramazda, 159.
Alexander, 31, 58, 211.
    feast of, 48.
Amalekites, Amalika, 147, 148.
Amarphal, Amarpal, 30.
Amestris, 164, 196, 197.
Ammon, salt of, 49.
Amu, 148.
Amyntas, 70.
Anaitis, temple of, 41.
Anthylla, 139.
Arabia, frankincense from, 58, 115.
Arabs, gift to the king, 248.
Ararat, 15.
Arbela, battle of, 12, 31.
Arbiter bibendi, 66.
Archilochus the Parian, 69.
Areus, 174.
Aria, 15.
Arioch, 30.
Aristagoras, 30.
Armenia, 15.
Arrian, 211.
Arrows of fate, 162.
Artabanus, 53, 142.

Artaxerxes, 91, 125, 141, 212.
Artaÿnta, 21, 195-198.
Artemisia, 19.
Ashdod, speech of, 95.
Ashtoreth, 111.
Asia Minor, 15.
Aspamistras, 142.
Assembly, 52.
Assos, 49.
Assurbanipal, 10.
    conquers Elam, 29.
Assyria, 9-11, 15, 115.
Astyages slays the son of Harpagus, 18.
    his dream, 88, 89.

Babel, tower of, 110.
Babylon, royal palace, 40.
    scenes in, 110.
Babylonia, 15.
Bactria, 15, 197.
Bagæus, 170.
Bagdad, 176.
Balowat gates, 142.
Banquet of wine, 49.
    date of the banquet at Shushan, 54.
Beauty, 117, 118.
    danger of, 121.
    definition of, 119.
    moral, 121, 122.
    of man, 120.
    queenliness of, 107.
    studied in the Orient, 130.
Beginning of the end, 224.
Behistun inscription, 87.
Bel, temple of, 110.
Belshazzar, feast of, 48.
Benefactors rewarded, 206-208.
Bigthan, Bigtha, 141.
Book of Esther drawn from official records, 230, 231.
    apocryphal, 255, 256.

258   BEAUTY CROWNED—INDEX.

Bowing in worship, 151, 152.
Brick-making in Chaldea and Babylonia, 229.
Brilliant entertainments, 46.

Callatebus, 163.
Cambyses, 179.
    marriage, 124.
    slays son of Prexaspes, 16.
    treatment of body of Amasis, 17.
Candaules, 68.
Cape Sepias, 164.
Captivity, 111–114.
Carthaginians, 51.
Caucasus, 248.
Celts, 51.
Chaldeans, priests, 160, 161.
Chamberlains, the seven, 67.
Chebar, 108.
Chedorlaomer, 29, 30, 147.
Chehl Minar, 34, 36.
China polyandry, 97, 98.
Choaspes, 31.
Cilicia, 206.
Cissia, 24.
City of lilies, 24.
Cleomenes, account of Susa, 30, 31.
Colchians, gifts to the king, 248.
Concubines, 99.
Confiscation of property, 224.
Conjugal relations in the Old Testament, 98.
Consecration to God, 126.
Conspiracy discovered, 141, 142.
    conspirators slain, 143.
Coprates, 31.
Cos, 158.
Cosmetics, 61.
Council of Trent, 98.
Court of a Persian king, 59.
Covering the head, 220–223.
Crœsus, 17.
Crown on horses, 215.
Ctesias, 42, 146.
Curntii, 220–222.
Curtius, 152.
Cuthæans, 40.
Cyaxares, 11, 89.
    slaughters the Scythians, 159.
Cyprus, 15.
Cyrus, 12, 18, 91, 114.

Dabhar, meaning of, 220.
Damocedes, 206.

Daniel, tomb of, 27, 32, 34.
    as pontiff, 43.
    dwelt at Shushan, 42.
Daris of Samos, 51.
Darius, 47, 58, 86, 87, 99, 151, 207, 224, 247.
Dascylus, 68.
David, 116.
Delhi, 176.
Demaratus, 211, 212.
Diodorus, 139, 185.
Dizfúl, 31.
Divination, 160, 161.
Dress, crime of wearing the king's, 211, 212.
Druses slaughter the Christians, 177.

Ecbatana, 41, 42.
Edict of Esther, 242, 243.
Edict of slaughter, 174, 175.
Education, 61.
Egypt, 15.
Ehud, 150.
Elam, 24, 30.
    meaning of word, 29.
Ellasar, 30.
Elymais, 24.
Eriaku, 30.
Esau, 148, 149.
Esdraelon, 150.
Estelle, 117.
Esther, 116.
    again pleads before the king, 225, 226.
    apparel, 136.
    appoints a fast, 188.
    appoints Mordecai administrator of Haman's property, 225.
    before the king, 194, 195.
    brought to the king's house, 123.
    character, 122.
    commendation, 137.
    consecrated to God, 126.
    difficulties, 190.
    faith, 189–191.
    favored by Hegai, 123.
    her edict, 242, 243.
    in the palace, 129.
    invites the king and Haman to a banquet, 198–200.
    kindred kept secret, 123, 124.
    meaning, 117.
    obedient to Providence, 126.

Esther—*continued.*
   patriotism, 226, 227.
   remembers her benefactor, 140.
   responsibility, 190.
   reveals relations to Mordecai, 224.
   reveals the plot, 217, 218.
   tomb, 254, 255.
   visits the king, 136.
   won the king, marriage, feast, 137, 138.
Ethiopians not taxed, 248.
Etiquette, 61, 184.
Eulæus, Ulaï, 27, 28.
Eunuch, meaning of word, 101.
   influence, 101, 102.
Executions, methods of, 142.
Exiles, 108.
   employments, 111.
   groups, 111.
   in Egypt, 115.
   number who returned, 114, 115.
   of Judah, 115.
Ezekiel, visions, 110, 119.
   mentions divination, 162.
Ezra, 115, 154.

Family, Persian, 102.
   Bible picture, 103.
   model, 102, 103.
   Xerxes', 103.
Fars, 14.
Fast of Esther, 189.
Feast, preparations for, 62, 63.
   deliberations, 65.
   food, 64.
   "no compelling," 66.
   scenes, 64, 65.
Flatterers, 83.
Footmen, 171.
Futteh Ali Shah, 202.

Gems, 61, 62.
Gera, 116.
Germans, 51.
Gifts to the king, 248.
Goïm, 30.
Golden bowl, 38.
Golden plane-tree, 38.
Golden vine, 38.
Grecian war, 106.
Grief, signs of, 177–180.
Guti, Gutium, 30.
Gyges, 12, 68.
Gyndes, 18.

Hadassah, 116, 117.
Hall of state, 43, 44.
   scene in, 61.
Haman, 44, 120, 121.
   casts lots, 166.
   character and government, 225, 226, 232.
   children, 201, 202.
   compelled to honor Mordecai, 212, 213.
   condemned, 220.
   despair, 219.
   discouraged by his friends, 216.
   great honors, 200.
   his sons impaled, 244.
   identifications, 150.
   impaled, 223.
   influence at court, 151.
   invited by Esther to a banquet, 199, 200.
   kingly honors, 210.
   loyal family, 203.
   names of his sons, 238.
   parades his fortune, 202, 203.
   pleads for his life, 219.
   pride, 154.
   property confiscated, 224.
   religion, 164.
   rises early, 208, 209.
   selfishness, 209, 210.
   unhappy, 203.
Hanging, 143.
Happiness not in worldly gifts, 84, 85, 203.
Harbonah, 223.
Harem, 105, 106.
Hatach, 181–185.
Hatra, palace of, 40.
Havilah, 147.
Hebrews, molten sea of the, 40.
Hegai, 123, 135.
Helbon, wine of, 49.
Hellespont scourged and branded, 18.
Hermotimus, 102.
Herod, 195.
Herodias, 195.
Herusha, 148.
Hezekiah, 9.
Home, 96.
   Christian, 103.
   symbol of heaven, 103.
Horatii, 220–222.
Hormah, battle of, 149.
Hur, 149.
Husbands, plurality of, 97, 98.

Iberians, 51.
Impalements, 142, 143.
    among the Turks, 143.
    by Darius, 143.
India, 15.
Influence, 93.
Inscriptions, 43.
    Behistun, 87.
Intaphernes, 183, 184.
Isaiah, 133.
Ispahan, 176.
Istar, 117.
Izdubar, 29.

Jair, 116.
Janizaries, 176.
Jehoiakim, captivity of, 107, 113.
Jeremiah, 111.
Jews in exile, 107.
    advantages, 113.
    defensive warfare, 238.
    may defend themselves against their enemies, 229-231.
    number of their enemies slain, 237, 238.
    organization in exile, 108, 109.
    patriotism and religion, 107.
    second day of their defense, 239, 240.
    struggle, 236, *et seq.*
    touch no spoil, 239, 240.
    victory, joy, and gladness, 240, *et seq.*
Joktanites, 147.
Josephus, 144.
Joshua, 149.
Judas Maccabæus, 189.
Jupiter, chariot of, 163.

Kerkhah, 31.
Khabour, 108.
Khan of Khiva, 142.
Khumbaba, 29.
King of Persia at table, 48.
    amusements, 49, 50.
    diadem, 55.
    dress, 55.
    fly-chaser, 57.
    his court, 59.
    luxuries of, 49.
    number of wives, 98.
    ornaments, 57.
    parasol, 56.
    scent bottle, 58.
    scepter, 56.

King's benefactors, 143-145.
King's duties, 145, 146.
Kish, 115.
Kislev, 137.
Kohl, 131.
Koords butcher the Nestorians, 177.
Kudur Mabug, 30.
Kudur Nakkhunti, 30.

Lacedæmonians, 138, 152.
Lake Moeris, 139.
Lampsacus, 206.
Larsa, 30.
Laws of Medes and Persians, 227, 228.
Legalized war, 236.
Leonidas, 86.
Letters of Mordecai hastened, 229.
Loftus, 34.
Lots, 165, 166.
Lucky and unlucky days, 165.
Lud, 147.
Luristan, mountains of, 24.
Lydia, 12.

Magabysus, 246.
Magi, mentioned in Bible, 159.
    influence over Cambyses, 161.
    massacred, 162.
    Pseudo-Smerdis, 161.
    rites, 162.
Magnesia, 206.
Mardonius, 19, 178.
Masistes, 21, 195-198.
Masistius, 178.
Massacres, 157, 158.
Medes, 157.
Media conquered, 12.
Megabazus, 70.
Memucan, 91, 92.
Mesabates, 91.
Mesha, 133.
Midianites, 150.
Milton, 31.
Miriam, 149.
Mithras, feast of, 51.
Mithridates gives Cyrus his first wound, 207.
Mithridates puts Italians to death, 158.
Mizraim, 147.
Moabites, 150.
Mohammed, 120.

BEAUTY CROWNED—INDEX. 261

Mordecai, 115.
    adopts Esther, 115, 116.
    bowed not, 153, 200, 221.
    care of Esther, 125.
    character, 116.
    charge to Esther, 181, 182.
    convinces Esther, 185, 186.
    fasts with the other Jews, 188.
    his grief, 177, 178.
    his robes and crown, 231-233.
    honored by the rabbis, 253, 254.
    honors await him, 212-215.
    made prime minister, 225.
    popularity of his administration, 233.
    position, 125.
    record read, 205.
    reveals the plot to Esther, 181, 182.
    speaks peace to the Jews, 253.
    suggested identifications, 245, 246.
    the king's benefactor, 146.
    to be hung, 203, 204, 208, 209.
    tomb of Mordecai and Esther, 254, 255.
    writes an edict in the king's name to save the Jews, 228.
Mourning, 177-180.
    not permitted in the royal palace, 180, 181.
Mousa, the Parthian queen, 70.

Nabopolassar, 11.
Nana, the goddess, 30.
Nebuchadnezzar, 11, 111.
    feast of, 48.
Nebuzaradan, 115.
Nehemiah, 95, 115, 154.
    at Shushan, 42.
Nereids, 164.
Nergal, 39.
Nestorians butchered, 177.
Nimrod, 29.
Nineveh, 15.
Ninip, 39.
Nisæan horses, 163.
Nisan, 166.
Nizir, 27.

Obedience to Providence, 126.
Œobazus, 86.
Official records, 230, 231.
Oriental hospitality, 46.
Oriental promises, 195-198.

Ornaments, 57.
    among the Midianites, 133.
    in Assyria and Babylonia, 134.
    in Chaldea, 134.
    in Media, 135.
    in Palestine, 131.
    in Persia, 134, 135.
    love of, rebuked, 133.
    Mishna, 133.
    number and variety, 132.
Oroetes, 170, 171, 224.
Orosangs, 144.
Osirtasen I., 169.
Otanes, 204.

Pactolus, 12.
Palace platform, 37.
    canopy and couches, 38.
    court of the garden, 44.
    difficulty of gaining entrance, 182-184.
    first house of the women, 44.
    furnishment, 37.
    king's palace, 44.
    queen's palace, 44, 45.
    throne, 39.
Palestine, 15.
Parasol, royal, 56.
Parmenio, 173.
Parsi, the modern, 160.
Parthian kings, 58.
Parysatis, 91, 139.
Pauline de Viguiere of Toulouse, 120.
Pausanius, 51, 145.
Pen, power of, 111.
Pentecost, 29.
Perfumeries, 59.
Pergamus of Priam, 163.
Persepolis, 36.
    inscriptions, 22, 23.
    treasures, 47.
Persia, extent of empire, 13.
    footmen, 171.
    inns, 172.
    Persia Proper, 14
    postal system, 172.
    post houses, 172.
    post routes, 173.
    provinces, 14.
    sacred books of, 159.
    soldiers, 172.
    swift riders, 172.
Persian empire, population, 237.
Persian gift, 196.

Persian king, crime of wearing his garments, 211, 212.
Persians, character of, 12, 13.
    dress, 60.
    drunkenness, 50.
    early temperance, 60.
    friendly to the Jews, 232, 233.
    power of their king, 13.
    riches of camp, 81, 82.
    sacrifice of prisoners, 164.
    sin of falsehood, 13.
    table customs, 50.
Persians and Medes, laws of, 91, 104, 105.
Phenicia, 15.
Philetas, 223.
Philotus, 173.
Phraataces, 70.
Plato, 51.
Pliny, 58.
Poetic justice, 216.
Pride before a fall, 147.
Property of enemies confiscated, 167, 168.
Prostration, 153.
Providence, 186–188.
Providential systems, 127.
Pseudo-Smerdis, 138.
    assassination of, 157, 207.
Purim, 243–245.
Pythius the Lydian, 38, 86.

Queen at meals, 70.
Queen-mother, authority of, 100.
Quintus Curtius, 99.

Rameses III., 148.
Records made by scribes, 145.
Religion of Persia, 158, 159.
    of Chaldea, 160.
Rephidim, battle of, 149.
Roads, 171.
Robes of honor, 231, 232.
Royal bounties, 139.
Royal judges, 124.

Sabaco, 169.
Sacans, 197.
Sacrifices to streams, 164.
    to winds, 89.
Salamis, 19, 144.
Samuel, 150.
Sanjur, king of Persia, 33.
Sardis, 106.
Sassanian king, court of, 80.
Satrapies, 248–252.
Saul, 116, 150, 185.
Scent bottle, 58.
Scepter, 56.
    forms of the, 185.
Scribes, 171.
Scythians, 51.
    slaughtered by Cyaxares, 157.
Seal, 168.
    of Darius Hystaspis, 169.
    of Joseph, 169.
    of Sennacherib, 169.
    ring seal, 169.
    symbol, 169, 170.
    use of, 168, 179.
Sebsewar, 176.
Second edict, 236, 237.
Seirites, 148.
Semites, cult, 162.
    gods, 162.
    planetary worship, 163.
    precepts of, 163.
Sennacherib defeats the Ethiopians and the Egyptians, 9.
Seven great families of Persia, 87.
    privileges of, 88.
Shaashgaz, 135.
Shapur, 27, 31, 43.
Shasu, 148.
Sheba, 115.
Sheikh Ali Mirza, 202.
Shimei, 116.
Shinar, 30.
Shur, 147.
Shush, 27.
    mounds of, 31.
Shushan, 15, 42.
    joy in, 232.
    palace of, 43, 123, 145.
    population, 237.
    the city, 42.
Shuster, 27.
Sin, 228.
Sivan, 228, 229.
Socrates, 189.
Solomon, 40, 60, 199, 208.
Soothsayers of Scythia, 161.
Stanley, 107.
Stella, 117.
Stones of pavement, 63.
Strabo, 44, 164.
Strymon, 164.
Sumir, 30.
Superstition and cruelty, 157.

Susa, 24, 30, 178.
    citadel mound, 43.
    city of, 27, 28.
    heat of, 29.
    inscriptions, 29.
    palace of, 34–37.
    present desolation, 32.
    riches, 31.
    the great platform, 43.
Susiana, 15.
    nature of the country, 25, 26.
    territory, 24.
Susis, 24.

Tacitus, 51.
Talmud, accounts in the, 154, 213–215.
Tamerlane, massacres of, 176.
Targum, 244.
Tebeth, month of, 137.
Temple of Bel, 110.
Ten tribes, the, 115.
Teresh, 141.
Teribazus, 212.
The wise men, 88.
Themistocles, 206.
Theodon the Samian, 38.
Thetis, 164.
Throne, 39.
Thucydides, 144.
Thurgal, 30.
Tidal, 30.
Tower of Babel, 110.
Tribute, 247, 248.
Trouble in the palace, 141.
Tur-gal, 30.
Turks, their slaughter of Christians, 176, 177.
Turn to be introduced to the king, 135.

Ulai, 27, 32.

Vashti, feast of, 67.
    disgraced, 104.
    disobeys the king, 82, 100.
    divorced, 95.
Virgins, 99.

Walpole, 120.
Ways, The Nine, 164.
Wife, 97.
    rank of, in Rome, 98.
Williams, General, 34.

Wine, 71, 72.
    as a medicine, 74.
    at the table, 74.
    Bible, 75.
    in the home, 73, 74.
    the curse of, 76.
Winged human-headed bulls and lions, 39.
Wheels within wheels, 205.
Woman, seclusion of, 100.
Writing, material, character, the pen, ink, 173.
    an ancient letter, 174.

Xerxes, 12.
    absolute power, 85.
    amours, 20, 21.
    assembly of, 52.
    character drawn by Rawlinson, 21.
    character fits Ahasuerus, 22.
    chronology of events, 23.
    could not forgive, 87.
    defeated at home, 85.
    diadem, 55.
    dream, 55.
    dress, 55.
    encourages hard drinking, 72.
    extent of empire, 22.
    extravagant promises, 197.
    fan or fly-chaser, 57.
    feared by Mardonius, 19.
    grants Mordecai and Esther authority to draw up letters to save the Jews, 227.
    his wrath, 83.
    inflamed with wine, 67.
    listens to the records, 205.
    love for wife of Masistes, 195–198.
    love of display, 51.
    makes a release to the provinces, 138.
    master of Athens, 178.
    murdered, 142.
    name, 22.
    obedience of Persians, 20.
    on his throne, 63.
    pacified, 223.
    palace, 44.
    rage against Haman, 218–220.
    rashness, 71.
    repents of rashness, 104.
    retreat from Europe, 19.

Xerxes—*continued*.
    royal parasol, 56.
    scepter, 56.
    scourges the Hellespont, 18.
    seeks advice, 53.
    selfish, 82.
    sends for Vashti, 70.
    shows his treasures, 66.
    slays his helmsman, 20.
    slays Phenician sailors, 19.

Xerxes—*continued*.
    spends a sleepless night, 205, 208.
    title, 22.
    war tent, 51.

Zedekiah, 111.
Zend-Avesta, 158.
Zeresh, 203.
Ziklag, 150.
Zoroastrian belief, 159, 160.

THE END.

www.ingramcontent.com/pod-product-compliance
Lightning Source LLC
Chambersburg PA
CBHW032143230426
43672CB00011B/2428